Kay Rosen

lifeli[k]e

Kay Rosen
lifeli[k]e

Organized by Cornelia H. Butler and Terry R. Myers

The Museum of Contemporary Art, Los Angeles
Otis Gallery, Otis College of Art and Design, Los Angeles

This publication accompanies the exhibition "Kay Rosen: *lifeli[k]e*," organized by Cornelia H. Butler and Terry R. Myers and presented at The Museum of Contemporary Art, Los Angeles, November 15, 1998 - February 14, 1999, and at Otis Gallery, Otis College of Art and Design, December 5, 1998 - February 14, 1999.

"Kay Rosen: *lifeli[k]e*" is made possible in part by The Andy Warhol Foundation for the Visual Arts, Inc., Lannan Foundation, and David Hockney. Additional support for the catalogue has been provided by Clayton Press and Gregory Linn.

Photo credits: frontispiece, Frank E. Hagenbuch; page 24 (right), Charles Mayer; page 27 (right), Tom Warren; pages 47, 55, 59, 80, James Prinz; page 49, Eric Pollitzer; pages 62, 68, John Geiser; pages 64, 72, Herbert Lotz; pages 65, 66, Donald Waller; pages 71, 81, Tom van Eynde; pages 73, 74, 75, Peter Muscato.

Copyright © 1998
The Museum of Contemporary Art, Los Angeles
250 South Grand Avenue
Los Angeles, California 90012
and
Otis Gallery, Otis College of Art and Design
9045 Lincoln Boulevard
Los Angeles, California 90045

ISBN 0-914357-68-9
Edited by Sue Henger and Jane Hyun
Designed by Catherine Lorenz
Printed by Color Service, Inc.

frontispiece:
HI, 1997/98
billboard, Route 15, Lewisburg, Pennsylvania
sponsored by Billboard Project, Center Gallery, Bucknell University

Contents

Lenders to the Exhibition

Bill Arning
Art:Concept, Paris
Bodi Collection
Laura Carpenter, Santa Fe, New Mexico
Mr. and Mrs. Robert J. Dodds III, Santa Fe, New Mexico
Ruth and Steve Durchslag
Galerie Friedrich, Bern
Anthony and Linda Grant, New York
Dr. Heinz Peter Hager, Bolzano, Italy
Alvin D. Hall, New York
Fredericka Hunter
Annette and Melvyn Klein
Helga Maria Klosterfelde, Hamburg
Anstiss and Ronald Krueck
Yvon Lambert, Montfauet, France
Micah Lexier, Toronto
Margo and Bob Marbut
Eileen and Peter Norton, Santa Monica
Mark Patsfall Graphics, Cincinnati
Private collection
Private collection. Courtesy Feature, Inc., New York
Private collection, Gary, Indiana
Private collection, London
Private collection, New Mexico
Private collection, Philadelphia
The Progressive Corporation, Cleveland, Ohio
Re Rebaudengo Sandretto, Torino
Refco Group, LTD., New York
Chula Reynolds
A.G. Rosen, Wayne, New Jersey
Kay Rosen
Rosenthal and Rosenthal, New York
Dr. James and Dorothy Stadler
Ginny Williams
Wooster Gardens, New York
Rosina Lee Yue

It is our great pleasure and honor to present, at MOCA and Otis Gallery, this twenty-five year survey of the paintings, wall paintings, photographs, public works, and ephemera of Kay Rosen, an artist of international reputation who lives and works in Gary, Indiana. The exhibition originated from the mutual interest shared by MOCA Associate Curator Connie Butler and Terry R. Myers, Associate Professor and critic-in-residence at Otis College of Art and Design. Both curators worked closely with the artist in developing the wide ranging scope of the exhibition and its catalogue.

It has been extremely gratifying to encourage and support this first collaboration between two great Los Angeles institutions, situated in such a manner that this exhibition is able to embrace a large part of the city. Otis Gallery has a long tradition of presenting challenging contemporary art by the best emerging and mature voices from Los Angeles and elsewhere. MOCA's history is based on providing a platform for the most innovative artists working today. The collaboration has made possible the distinct nature of "Kay Rosen: lifeli[k]e"— one exhibition composed of two complementary but distinct and complete installations which, together, give a complete view of the artist's multifaceted oeuvre.

Such an exhibition involves many dedicated individuals without whose energy and commitment it would not have been possible. First we thank Connie Butler and Terry R. Myers for a collaborative spirit and intelligence that brought this project to fruition.

At Otis, we thank Jinger Heffner, Otis Exhibitions Coordinator, who also functions as registrar and preparator. We are indebted to Tone O. Nielsen, the exhibition's primary research and technical assistant, who provided critical support at all stages, especially with the public projects that are a vital component of the exhibition. Appreciation also goes to Nancy Forest Brown, Otis' inspired Director of Grants Management.

For their committed support of this collaboration, we offer special thanks to Bronya Galef, Chairman of the Otis Board of Trustees, the Board of Trustees itself, and Neil Hoffman, President of Otis College of Art and Design.

At MOCA, Curatorial/Editorial Secretary Jane Hyun was instrumental in coordinating the publication materials and other aspects of the exhibition. MOCA Registrar Robert Hollister and Assistant Registrar Portland McCormick coordinated all shipping arrangements for the exhibition, and Exhibitions Production Manager John Bowsher and his exceptional staff are responsible for realizing its handsome installation. Director of Development

Erica Clark provided support as did Facilities and Operations Director Randy Murphy. Additionally we thank Assistant Director Kathleen Bartels, Chief Curator Paul Schimmel, and Director of Education Kim Kanatani for their support of the exhibition.

We gratefully acknowledge Audrey M. Irmas as Chair, Gilbert B. Friesen as President, Lenore S. Greenberg as Program and Exhibition Liaison, and the entire MOCA Board of Trustees for their unending commitment and support.

Our deep appreciation also goes to several key individuals whose dedication was crucial. Catherine Lorenz, as always, brought sensitivity and care to the unique design of this publication. Norm Laich, whose impressive work caught the artist's eye many years ago, provided unequaled expertise to the execution of the wall paintings. Tom Ladd of AIDS Project Los Angeles (APLA) energetically engineered a new version of Rosen's bus project, providing for the recontextualization of an earlier, yet still germane, public work. We are grateful to Lynne Sowder, Curator, and Nancy Monda, Director of Camel Work In Progress, R.J. Reynolds Tobacco Company, for their support of the exhibition. On behalf of the artist we are happy to acknowledge Bud Rosen, James Kelly, Adam Brooks, Jean Crutchfield, Hudson, Michael Jenkins, Tim Porges, Brent Sikkema, and Stuart Horodner.

We gratefully thank the lenders to the exhibition without whose generous participation the exhibition would not have been possible. The exhibition and its catalogue received significant support from The Andy Warhol Foundation for the Visual Arts, Inc., Lannan Foundation, and David Hockney. Additional support for the catalogue is provided by Clayton Press and Gregory Linn. We appreciate their vision and commitment to this project.

Finally, our deepest thanks go to Kay Rosen, whose challenging and generous work inspires us to look and read, read and look, with greater attention and awareness. It has been exceedingly gratifying to work with her and bring this distinguished body of twenty-five years of work to a broader audience.

Anne Ayres   Richard Koshalek
Director, Otis Gallery   Director, MOCA

the forest for the trees
Cornelia H. Butler

There exists a loosely configured art history of the American Midwest comprising artists who use text. Perhaps only in the curatorial imagination, it seems that an eccentric line might be drawn connecting Marsden Hartley, Robert Indiana, Bruce Nauman, Mike Kelley, and Kay Rosen. Based on Mike Kelley's felt banners with high school slogans reworked for full irony and lowbrow humorous effect, one could speculate about growing up a creative child in middle America and the need to come to terms with one's white roots amidst mall and fast-food culture. Given Robert Indiana's quoting of Charles Demuth's famous *Figure Five in Gold*, a painted homage to William Carlos Williams's poem of the same name, one might think of the mythology of the railroad, connecting east and west, and the random encounter with public text in the form of billboards and highway signs. Personalizing pop art's appropriation, the younger Indiana was so enamored of his Midwestern roots that he adopted the name of his home state as his own. Bruce Nauman's manipulation of vernacular text often has a folksy quality not usually associated with life in big cities.[1] Unscientifically juxtaposed, these artists share a restless interest in the colloquial and a genuine core of populist intentionality.

When, in 1978, Kay Rosen made the photo-grid titled *A Song and Dance*, which documented and transformed a performative exercise into a work of tremendous formal and social power, it was remarkable for several reasons. Perhaps the fact that this early work and, for that matter, all of Rosen's work is made in Gary, Indiana, is only extraordinary to those of us who don't live there. The vast territory between the coasts hardly registers in the commercial art world. We seem to understand the Midwest as a place where great artists come from. Chicago, a fifty-minute train ride northwest of Gary, is Rosen's adopted art community. In fact, she and her husband Bud, whom she met while attending Newcomb College, a women's college that shares a campus with Tulane University, live in Miller, a beachfront town annexed to Gary in 1918. A steel mill town with a tumultuous political history, Gary almost collapsed under the weight of its own economic and social struggles in the wake of the exodus of its white middle-class citizens after the election of Mayor Richard Hatcher in 1968. After Flint, Michigan, Gary was the second city in the United States to elect a black mayor. Kay recalls the saturation of "for sale" signs around the city and the organized effort by the city to prohibit them.

Miller also suffered in the wake of this shift but has since thrived as a small town of mixed ethnicity and political strength. Kay and Bud live, as they have for twenty-eight years, in a one-story, ranchstyle house on the edge of Lake Michigan, so close you

Figure 1
Kay Rosen
The Exhibition, 1978 (detail)
black and white photograph

can hear the waves. Kay works in a wood-paneled studio in the basement. On the way to and from the train station, you pass Gateway Park, the site of a project in which the artist and a friend made a series of walks among the columns of a gazebo (which still exists). As you pass, Kay points out the sign that barely marks the traffic triangle the park has become.

What is important about mentioning all this, framing Kay's work in terms of the extremely "normal" environment in which it is made, aside from the unavoidable exoticism of the whole experience to the jaded visitor from either coast, is that Kay has chosen to remain in this context, raise a family and make art in part because of Miller's natural beauty, but also because of her social commitment to and history with the place. It's easy to get nostalgic about the pictures of Rosen and her friends out in the landscape—artists in blue jeans and black—making simple performances combining pedestrian movement and linguistic exercise, elaborating the conceptualist legacy that has become so important and so mythologized for the current generation of art students and art historians. But these early experiments, movements and conceptual exercises are also crucial to an understanding of the origins of the artist's work (Fig. 1).

Rosen received a graduate degree in languages and linguistics. Feeling limited by the academic study of language, she almost immediately began making drawings based on many of the ideas about structure she had studied in comparative or applied linguistics. Growing up in Corpus Christi, Texas, where Spanish was spoken as commonly as English—the names of white suburban streets often had bastardized Spanish ("spanglish") names—and where one of her grandmothers spoke only Yiddish, she was acutely aware of the social potential of language and the slippage that occurs at the border of two cultures.

In Chicago during the early 1970s, the dance community was active, and spaces such as Moming provided a platform for experimental dance, music and performance by such artists as Steve Reich, Trisha Brown and Lucinda Childs. Rosen cites these artists as influences and was interested in their relationship to minimalism; minimalist painting and sculpture didn't interest her at the time. Experiments with so-called objective dance and other postmodern movement strategies evolved out of Black Mountain College in North Carolina and the Judson Church in New York City between the late 1950s and early 1970s. The linguistic roots of performance and dance at this time can be seen in Rosen's diagrammatic photo works, which followed in the years immediately after the revolutionary work of choreographers such as Yvonne

Rainer, Brown and Childs. Just a few years before, Rainer made *Trio A* (1967), a stark, groundbreaking, single phrase of movement employing minimalism's reductive vocabulary to investigate the economy and form of pedestrian gesture exquisitely composed on the body of the dancer (Fig. 2).

Perhaps even more directly influential on Rosen's work was Steve Reich's *Writings About Music* (1974), which expanded the experience of listening, and linguistically based compositions such as "It's Gonna Rain," recorded in 1965.[2] This moving and quite political language-based work excerpts the voice of a black Pentecostal preacher, Brother Walter, sermonizing about the end of the world. His voice is looped in and out of phase with multiple tracks of the same text fragment until a kind of controlled chaos takes over. In 1966 Reich composed a piece titled "Come Out" from the voices of six boys arrested for murder during the Harlem riots of 1964. The cataclysmic beauty of "It's Gonna Rain" and the subtle but irrepressible way it insinuates itself into the consciousness of the listener are shattering when first experienced. It was this kind of operation performed on found text that impressed Kay as she was making the transition away from academia and finding visual form for her interest in the structure, texture, and infinite mutability of letters, words, and their meaning.

Works such as Rosen's *Gateway Park, Gary, Indiana II* (1980) and *Hyde Park, Chicago, Illinois II* (1980) were made using similarly elementary strategies. The residual photo works are a telling combination of existing architectural structure, the intervention of human form and the abstract diagram that tracks the result of the action. Extrapolated from Rosen's linguistic studies, this equation of the vernacular reworked and re-presented is the operation she would perform in her primary body of work as a visual artist—her paintings—from 1985 to the present. It is worth noting Rosen's subtle comparison between Chicago's Hyde Park area around the University of Chicago—now populated by a mixed community of university types and African-American working class, its grand colonnade a reminder of its wealthy urban past—and its counterpart, the little folly of a rotunda in Gary's Gateway Park. Perhaps a commentary on the idea of the satellite city or, more probably, a wry retake on Robert Smithson's forays into the hinterlands of New Jersey, it also is available to us only via gritty black-and-white photographs and apocryphal art lore. In either case, Rosen's interest in the highly conceptual, reductive gesture mixed with a strong political longer view has continued to drive her work (Fig. 3).

Figure 3
Kay Rosen
Double Staircase, 1978 (detail)
black and white photographs

With this in mind, it is worth looking more closely at the earlier *Changing Seats* (1978), which, like *Brides and Slinkies Descending the Staircase* (1977), was made for a group exhibition at Moming, Chicago's version of New York's Judson Church.[3] This work involved five people moving progressively forward through five rows of three seats each. Like a stop-action flip book, the tiny heads at the back occupy the front seats in the end. The mixed ethnicity of the performers seems more than incidental, and the back-of-the-bus reference must be seen in terms of the racial tension in Gary at the time—a kind of "if you could walk a mile in their shoes." The simple orchestration of the sitters neutralizes any possible hierarchy in their positions within the progression of chairs and their relationship to each other. Just people, facing forward, staring out, moving through the exercise. Rosen maintains a commitment to what she calls the "ethics" of a work, which she locates in the balanced correspondence between the form and sense of the language she is using.[4] This ethical code developed out of the early work and Rosen's sense of the matching of movement at its most elemental with the system that is used to execute it. The seats in *Changing Seats* reinforce the underlying social implications of the work. What begins as improvisation becomes a complete paragraph of visual information.

Similarly, *A Song and Dance*, made for an exhibition titled "Daley's Tomb," curated by Jerry Saltz for N.A.M.E. Gallery the same year, is the work in which the artist locates the genesis of the relationship between movement and text. It focuses on a dancer's feet in the act of making and mimicking the positions of classical ballet. The text underneath mocks the malapropisms of Chicago's Mayor Daley, the song and dance of public oratory. The first line is taken directly from a book of Daley's renowned misapplications. As the talk dissolves into blather, so the structure of the cliché mutates into the undeniable truth. The structure of the dance is undermined and exposed and the language is further polluted by its own silly artifice to the point of nonsense.

> Together we must rise to ever higher and higher platitudes.
> Together we must rise to ever higher and higher plaid tutus.
> Together we must rise to ever higher and higher pas de deux.
> Together we must rise to wave a higher and higher pomp adieu.
> Together we must rise to wave a higher and higher pom pon too.

Together we must rise to have a high heir in our pomp endure.

Together we must rise to have our high hair attired in a pompadour.

Together we must rise to have our high hair entowered as a pontiff adored.

Together we must rise like high errant befoulers from the pot of Pandora.

Together we must rise like icarian fliers of the Audubon order.

Together we must rise like augurian fighters of the "ought to ban" order.

Together we must rise like a current of hot air from a mountebank orator.

Together we must rise like a Kyrien "Pater" from the mouths of Bach choristers.

Together we must rise like a hair-raising blunder from a malaprop character.

Made in socially inscribed spaces such as Moming—a strategy that Rosen refers to as "throw-away spaces as prompts"[5]—these performative works and the *Stairwalking* diagrams that followed not only activated space with movement, which the artist sees as the most direct form of intervention, but also delineated the evolution of an elementary vocabulary based on the slippage of meaning inherent in any formal language. Bruce Nauman's early studio actions, which exist as videotapes, such as *Walk with Contrapposto* or *Wall Floor Positions*, both from 1968, also employed reductive pedestrian movement or recontextualized ways of arranging the body as the simplest way to make meaning from nothing. The classical sculptural device of contrapposto, which throws the hips to one side, indicating the grounding and weight of a sculptural form, is reenacted by Nauman, who capitalized on the body's potential for signification.

Nauman's career-long involvement with language can also be seen in relationship to Rosen's project. Often employing puns, one-liners and clichés in his early work, Nauman was influenced by his teachers Robert Arneson and William T. Wiley. What Robert Storr describes as Nauman's knack at playing "dumb" to focus on words that "smart" is analogous to Rosen's use of deceptively simple strategies and rules to move the words and their meaning around: "These are one-liners, but like the best of the genre they are memorable because they turn on a logical dime without any wasted effort. So doing, they permanently inconvenience future use of the clichés they parody."[6] The movement in Nauman's early word plays—finding the palindrome or performing operations of reversal or exaggeration—parallels Rosen's. What becomes for Nauman a natural move into neon, Rosen eventually works into her paintings through color, typeface, and scale (Fig. 4).

In her text for the Zurich based magazine *du* (reprinted elsewhere in this volume) Rosen discusses the constructs imposed upon her and her work and describes herself in the following way: ". . . a (1) woman who (2) paints (usually) (3) small (usually) (4) images of language (mostly English), which because of their authorship, content, size, and process lie neither within historically validated categories of painting nor within historically validated categories of linguistics." That Rosen became a painter, an artist working on the flat surface of the canvas or the wall, follows from what is her obvious love of the words themselves, their form as well as their content. She talks about being influenced by such artists as Larry Rivers, his use of letters and how they look. Rivers's incorporation of words into his paintings anticipated the pop interest in text lifted from such banal cultural sources as billboards, the newspaper, and other public text. In their painterly mix of brushy color and stenciled letters, Rosen's five 1972 drawings in the exhibition clearly owe a debt to Rivers but also reference Jasper Johns's use of the readymade text (Fig. 5).

After a hiatus from language, a kind of self-imposed art schooling in which she experimented with sculpture and photo and notational performances, Rosen returned to the predominant use of text in 1982 with the series titled *Lines on Lines*, which also became the

basis for her first artist's book of the same name. Her second book *Mined* remains unpublished but contains a fold out which generated the 1983 work *No Noose Is Good Noose*. *No Noose* simultaneously occupies the space of the viewer while moving confidently into the space of painting. Incorporating much of the movement from earlier diagrammatic works into its physical and formal structure, Rosen uses the idea of revolution to propel the work forward from left to right. The stick figures, which evolve directly out of the coded marks of the *Stairwalking* works, animate the political morality tale that questions the efficacy of revolution and progress. Rosen uses the circle (as geometric figure, as clockface, as wheels, as heads, as noose) and language ("loophole," "whole loop," "whollop") to construct and drive the argument and to move the figures through different stations, positions, and roles. Using nine plexiglass and masonite panels colored only with black, white, and gray, Rosen makes explicit reference to political broadsheets or newsprint, now primitive forms of information dissemination.

       Like *No Noose*, Rosen's paintings from 1984-85 are physically less like traditional paintings than a sign-painter's mock-ups for a billboard and, indeed, they have on occasion functioned in this way for her. The whole series is about hearing, seeing, and speaking no evil and warns against turning a blind eye toward the abuse of power. Or, in the words of the artist, the demise of enlightenment: censorship; the gender/culture/race debate; unrequited or thwarted love in the age of AIDS; subjective and objective vision; misunderstanding arising from bilingual mishaps; and egregious acts. These paintings have been exhibited individually and, in some instances, as wall paintings with a mutability that underscores the artist's interest in the social implications of her work and a savvy eye for context. Brought together as a grid for this exhibition, the whole array is primarily black, white and dayglo red—what's black and white and red all over? The artist urges us not to trust everything we see in print.

       For example, the three-paneled *Blub, Blub, Blub*, originally made in 1985, was executed as a large-scale wall painting at the Contemporary Arts Center in Cincinnati, Ohio, in 1989, the same year the Mapplethorpe exhibition was rerouted through the Midwest in the wake of its obscenity controversy. The image of the light bulb sinking under the blubber of official speech became a symbol of free speech going under. *Alabama*, a more complex work also executed as a wall painting, mixes signifiers of race and gender.[7] Spelled phonetically, the "blahnd" leading the "blahnd" is illustrated by two female stick figures, one black and one white. The white blonde's identity is her own. She is empowered to dye her hair or assume another's role, but the black blonde's identity is fixed according to codes of institutionalized repression: "Some Canes Are Able, Some Ain't. Some Cain, Some Cain't." The blind circularity of race relations and power in America as represented by Alabama, seat of the civil rights movement, is perfectly articulated or, unarticulable, in Rosen's hands. The frustration that the viewer/reader encounters in appre- hending the shifting readings of the work mimics and mocks the real-life dilemma of race in the United States, where white and black brothers and sisters can't seem to just get along; the problem is stupidly simple yet dauntingly complex. This ability to hard-boil a hopelessly charged and complicated issue is classic Kay Rosen. It is the residue of the dispute between the linguistic and the visual that gives the work its tension.

As we begin to reconsider the 1980s, the decade during which Rosen's work began to reach a wider audience, it seems clear that a group of women artists emerged whose work was received and interpreted in a way that divorced it from its conceptualist and feminist roots.[8] The work of such artists as Barbara Kruger or Cindy Sherman was framed almost exclusively in terms of film or photographic theory. Comparing Rosen's treatment of issues of race and gender construction with her image/text contemporaries such as Kruger, Holzer, or Lorna Simpson reveals widely differing positions in relationship to formal considerations, content, and the location of the artist's voice. Jenny Holzer deploys an imperative and rather haunted poetic voice that often implores the viewer. In her public work she maintains a distanced, neutral voice even as she proclaims subjective realities in the public realm. Simpson's eloquent early black-and-white work relies on a certain poetic association between the minimal text and the culturally charged image. The deceptively simple text, usually in the form of one or two words, suggests different associations based on the viewer's cultural relationship to the images and iconic words.

Quoting Gilles Deleuze and Félix Guattari—"the elementary unit of language . . . the order-word . . . is not meant to be believed but to be obeyed"—critic Mark Van de Walle, in considering Rosen's work, states that "Much of the fashionable feminist language art in the 1980s took this dictum to heart and tried to monkeywrench the system of signs with 'subversive' order-words which couldn't be obeyed, or which tried to expose the wretchedness of authority by using the voice of authority . . . Rosen though manages to dodge the bullet."[9] Van de Walle laments what he perceives as a lack of irony and an abundance of moral superiority in commodity culture and in certain text-based work during the eighties. To whatever extent this is true, it is undeniable that Rosen, in her succinct, charged canvases, embraces the banal and indulges in the vernacular, and always in what appears to be a third-person voice. Oddly, it is Kruger's or Holzer's first person that is somehow less personal, more omniscient and wants to speak for all of us. Because there is no image accompanying Rosen's language, it requires a different kind of attention than Kruger's work. Unlike Jenny Holzer's often theatrical compositions, Rosen's poetry is unconventional, the unpredictable result of her manipulation of the word form and the viewer's act of reading. Text is not exploited as one device in the service of an image nor as a hybrid of both. Words are doggedly studied, massaged, manipulated, altered and re-presented in such a way that you find yourself imagining what it's like to be in Kay's brain.

With the rigor of an archivist, she keeps notes on words and phrases that might eventually succumb to her light but definitive touch. Kay places herself in the role of magician or medium. The "tah dah" she performs exploits, with a sleight of hand, the potentiality already embedded in her subjects. In early political works such as *Bam, Boo*, which

My father was never home, he was always drinking booze. He saw a sign saying DRINK CANADA DRY. So he went up there.

refers to Cuba, or *The Mexican Revolution* and *Border Peece*, which deal with Central and South America, one experiences an "I told you so" as the artist's meaning and vigilance become clear. Rosen stands at a distance and points us in the direction of the obvious.

In other works, such as the more recent *Oh, Eau* (1989/92), the narrative voice itself becomes the subject. By moving the punctuation in one paragraph and representing its slightly altered version beside it, Rosen sets the reading in flux. Like the readers of some foreign language Dick-and-Jane narrative, we ricochet between the two stories, which become inseparable: one is a passive tale of a broken heart and a deluge of drowned sorrows, the other is an active account of a rainstorm. A less theatrical manipulation than Reich's incantory "It's Gonna Rain", Rosen's double entendre *Oh, Eau* recalls the first lesson of acting: a change in intonation can radically alter the drama. This drama is carried out on the wall, with two very different scenes and kinds of dramatic tension conjured in the mind of the viewer.[10]

Kay is also very funny. When her distinctly antiheroically scaled paintings emerged in the overblown art world of the mid-1980s, it was startling and often hilarious to encounter them in a gallery or museum exhibition. Unlike much of the monochromatic image/text work of that moment, Rosen's subversive icons indulged in lowbrow, synthetic color. In the presence of a gallery exhibition of her work, one had the feeling that the artist was somehow inside the wall behind the work or chuckling in the corner with us. Shown at Feature throughout the 1980s, her work was in the company of such artists as Charles Ray, whose own sly sense of humor similarly warped the unassuming exhibition space. As when encountering his fabulously power-suited Pink Lady for the first time, Rosen's linguistic chunks of color on the wall hold the space in a loopy way.

Humor is difficult for any artist to pull off. Historically for women artists, pre-Roseanne Barr and Rosie O'Donnell, it was nearly *verboten*. Thinking back on Richard Prince's joke paintings of the late 1980s, for example, which Rosen greatly admires, there is no question that their provenance in the language of masculinity and feminist backlash is part of what legitimizes them and gives him permission (Fig. 6). Work by a woman artist making similar references—Sue Williams comes to mind, though her work is also tragic and comes from lived experience—is considered raunchy and hard to look at. Barbara Kruger has been considered too righteous when she effectively flips off the hegemony of gender relations. Or consider Jenny

tē āch
dub'l-ū
ā är tē

Holzer's ironic but deadly serious *Abuse of Power Comes as No Surprise*. It's O.K. to laugh at appropriated watercooler humor because of the ironic distance from the source. (David Letterman can get away with a tremendous amount of racism because he plays the nerdy white guy in a Times Square world of immigrants.) Mike Kelley's installation in the exhibition "Helter Skelter," titled *Mike Kelley's Proposal for the Decoration of an Island of Conference Rooms (with Copy Room) for an Advertising Agency Designed by Frank Gehry* (1991), is again an example of the artist embracing white, middlebrow culture as a kind of license to be perverse. Certainly part of his brilliance as an artist has been to hit this note over and over again either through text or through his sculptural stand-ins for his own adolescence. One is hard pressed to find a woman artist to whom humor is a central part of her practice. A woman artist must make herself into a caricature in order to succeed at this.[11]

So, when in 1988 Kay made the painting *Six*, which bore the text "Tworkov, Twombly, Twomen," it was a sly, inside joke at the art world's expense: two master painters, two men, two anonymous women working alongside them. Perfectly summing up the dilemma, the more subtle reading is "work, womb, women." Or consider the 1987 "stacked" painting titled after French painter Edgar Degas, whose art historical reputation as a misogynist can't be lost on Kay: she takes the shared letters of his first and last names and remakes him into a sort of Brooklyn thug: "Edga Dega."[12] In *Various Strata*, made as a painting in 1986 and again as a wall painting in 1996, the reference to institutionalized power is forceful yet humorous when Rosen editorializes in the final cadence of the work: "Him, Hymm, Hmmm." She sits underneath this pile of declined "h's" and "m's" and rattles the cage from below. A later work titled *She-Man* reverses the sanctified order by pointing out that within every strong woman is a man: "She, He, Her." In a reverse fairy-tale ending, the *he* has been eaten by the *she*. The underlying "he, he, he" that anchors the vertical stack of letters is again the artist having the last laugh.

Like *Edgar Degas*, other of the so-called stacked paintings Rosen made in the mid-1980s capitalize on her liberal sense of intellectual misbehaving with cultural history's cast of characters. Through typeface and color she performs a kind of drag on her subject in works such as *Georgy, Porgy, Bess* or *Go on, Goon*, and often focuses on archetypal male heroes and villains such as John Wilkes Booth, and Noah, as in the ark. *The "Ed" Paintings* (1988), a confounding narrative of biblical proportions, introduces two characters: a puffed-up hero named

Ed and his linguistic counterpart, -ed, the suffix of the past-tense verb, created by the justified right-hand margin. The artist's plot summary reads like a Hollywood "treatment":

> The action is propelled by the linguistic events, rather than by the dramatic ones, making the circumstances of the plot murky. It is known, however, that the narrative involves two women, Rosa and Blanch, another man, Mike, two (possibly four) deaths (possible murders), and resurrection, all condensed into the five "chapters" that comprise the work. The linguistic episodes concern duality as well: verbs acting as proper nouns and proper nouns, as verbs ("Surprise!"); look-alike words and sounds created by homonyms, repeated syllables, and stuttering ("Technical Difficulties" and "Sp-spit it Out"); and double meanings ("Blanks"). Implied by the deaths of Mike's microphone and of Ed are two linguistic casualties: the now silent, unamplified voice and the inefficacy of language (Ed's riddle). But the final panel suggests that after death there is life, because the story has been recorded by memory, on tape ("memorx"), and of course in writing.[13]

The sense that the artist can't help herself, that dishing is just part of being Kay Rosen working in the wood-paneled basement with an alphabet she knows inside and out, is shared by other irreverent language-based artists such as Jessica Diamond, Larry Johnson, and the writer Gary Indiana. For Diamond and Johnson humor often functions through exaggeration or a kind of out-of-the-corner-of-the-mouth understatement. Diamond too, for example, disses the art world and its treatment of women. In an ongoing homage to Yayoi Kusama, she manipulates the shape and emphasis of certain quotes from the artist and, in monumental, gregarious wall paintings, mixes these with wildly colored, abstracted references to her imagery. Johnson's wickedly smart, inside Hollywood jokes, juxtaposed with icons of L.A. kitsch that function as linguistic units in the presence of his text, are indulgent, arch, and raucously funny, if you get the jokes. Rather than prompting the knowing guffaw, Rosen's work illicits a slower smile because the operation of her work appears simpler in its execution but is often edgier and open to individual interpretation. The paintings continue to reverberate after you look away. The reading is the thing.

In 1992, Rosen made the thirteen paintings which became *Corpus*, literally a body which invokes autobiography, the too soon proclaimed death of the author, and the voice of authority. The artist indulges in color here, making a group of little rectangular, pink, red, and fleshy dashes which are somehow visceral when seen together. As in the 1996 drawing *Bleed*, in which the red ink seeps through the paper forming the letters of the word "wound," which are read (red) from the other side, the *Corpus* paintings economize their means. Since *Corpus* Rosen has performed more subtle articulations in which the manipulation of typeface or spacing upsets the usual reading. Works such as *Deaf, Still Life, Trickknees*, and *Double Whammy*, all made in 1993, riff on pedestrian types or genres of the superfamiliar. These paintings are small in scale and get their message across in one or two syllables. *Deaf*, a painted one-liner that appropriates the slang rap term meaning cool, also references the recording label Def Jam and manages a sly comment on what really loud music can do to uninitiated listeners. By slipping into the shorthand language of urban kids, this great little brown painting holds its own with the encoded language of wide sneakers or baggy shorts. *Still Life*, the last genre painting, declares itself in friendly, Hawaiian Punch pink and yellow. In mixing the uppercase letters with the two lowercase but tall "i"s, the art-historical bowl of fruit laughs at itself with its silly maraschino cherries on top. It's the campy, lowbrow, plastic version of its self-serious cousin. "Fruit" and "dish" are both hyperfemme words for gay men and women, which seem endearing in their compound state.

In the end, part of what fascinates Rosen is the possibility of using the tools of language and reading to undermine the very structures they concretize. The sense of amused confusion that one feels in the attempt at wrapping one's mind around a Kay Rosen is precisely where the tension and the moment of reckoning lie. In 1989 Rosen made a black-and-beige work titled *t-h-w-a-r-t* (Fig.7). The agony of attending to the phonetic spelling of the letters of the word "thwart," which becomes "teach double art," is the unexpected by-product of this confusion. Double talk is the metaphor for what's wrong with institutionalized art education.[14] In the pedantic "just let me spell it out for you" lies the obfuscation that pre-occupies her.

Like all good artists, Rosen works with a full command of history and theory but gets her hands dirty with her medium, the language itself. Not having attended art school, Rosen may see with a clearer eye. Trained as a linguist who chose not to get mired in French theory of the moment, she became intrigued with the investigation of the cultural possibilities for language through the subversion of its basic structure, form, and appearance. In a beautiful wall painting titled *The Forest for the Trees* (1990), a horizontal band of deep green, sans serif, italicized letters stutters out the letters that make up the cliché and the title of the work: "tthhee ffoorrreeesstt." Making a dense landscape at eye level in the standard space of painting, the cluster of letters hypnotizes as it spreads across the wall. Rosen revels in the dual challenge of dealing with language and its context, the foreground and periphery. Deep forest, deep consciousness, deep sleep, we are caught in the delightful, confusing moment of trying to see the forest and the trees.

Notes

1. Bruce Nauman was born in Fort Wayne, Indiana.

2. Steve Reich, *Writings About Music* (New York: Nova Scotia College of Art and Design with New York University Press, 1974). "It's Gonna Rain" and "Come Out" are featured on the recording *Early Works* (Electra/Nonsuch, New York, 1987).

3. *Brides and Slinkies Descending the Staircase* was made for an exhibition titled "All Over the Place", curated by Eileen Shukofsky, and *Changing Seats* was made for an exhibition titled "Paper Dolls" curated by Stan Trecker. Both took place at Moming Dance Center, Chicago.

4. Kay Rosen, "LIFELI[K]E," forthcoming in Stanley Tigerman, ed., *Archeworks: Morality and Ethics* (New York: The Monacelli Press, 1999).

5. From a discussion with the artist, August 14, 1998.

6. Robert Storr, "Beyond Words," in Kathy Halbreich and Neal Benezra, eds., *Bruce Nauman* (Minneapolis and Washington, D.C.: Walker Art Center in association with the Hirshhorn Museum and Sculpture Garden, Smithsonian Institution, 1994), 47-66.

7. The wall painting *Alabama* was part of an exhibition titled "Messages From the Interior," curated by Tim Porges for N.A.M.E. Gallery, Chicago, 1985.

8. Laura Cottingham mentions Kay Rosen and briefly introduces this issue in her essay, "Beyond the Seventies: The Impact of Feminist Art," in *The Power of Feminist Art: The American Movement of the 1970s, History and Impact* (New York: Harry N. Abrams, Inc., 1994), 282.

9. Mark Van de Walle, "Kay Rosen, Laura Carpenter Gallery," *THE Magazine* (October 1992): 17.

10. Lorna Simpson's recent film work operates in a similar way. In works such as *Call Waiting* (1997) the narratives are inconclusive and the action occurs off camera. Any reading of the action or promise of resolution is located solely in the intonation or attitude of the actor and the projection of the viewer.

11. Witness the career of Louise Bourgeois, whose own charming raunchiness and amazing body of work has only been fully appreciated and embraced now that the artist is in her eighties. Humor is posited more often in sculpture through the associative and metaphoric power of materials. I am thinking of the work of such artists as Jessica Stockholder, Katharina Fritsch, Liz Larner, and Rita McBride.

12. Rhonda Lieberman discusses Rosen's identity and the Jewishness of her humor in "Recent Painting by Jewish Woman in Indiana," *Art · Text*, no. 46 (September 1993): 54-59. For another discussion of Jewish humor, see Carla Johnson's "Luckless in New York: The Schlemiel and the Schlimazel in *Seinfeld*," *Journal of Popular Film and Television* 22 (Fall 1994): 116-124.

13. From a text by the artist written to accompany *The Ed Prints*, a portfolio of silkscreen prints based on the paintings and published by Volatile, Cincinnati, in 1992.

14. Rosen has taught at The School of The Art Institute of Chicago (home away from home of the real Edgar Degas) for many years.

Sounding out Kay Rosen
Terry R. Myers

And so now one finds oneself interesting oneself in an equilibration, that of course means words as well as things and distribution as well as between themselves between the words and themselves and the things and themselves, a distribution as distribution. This makes what follows what follows and now there is every reason why there should be an arrangement made. Distribution is interesting and equilibration is interesting when a continuous present and a beginning again and again and using everything and everything alike and everything naturally simply different has been done.
— Gertrude Stein, "Composition as Explanation"[1]

Like everything else, words should have a *value*, which is different from meaning; it is the speaker in them, waiting to be found. I have friends with whom I talk as though words had a *price*.

Price and meaning are both representations, imposed on the object from without by various economies of capital or language. Both fix the object in a demonstrative stasis, displaying it divorced from the marks of its development in time. Value is not strictly a representation but the articulation of an essence, not an imposition but a revelation from within of the true form of the object. As with any natural thing, one must partake a little of the mystical to understand it.
— Scott Long, "The Loneliness of Camp"[2]

JACK. Well, I won't argue about the matter. You always want to argue about things.
ALGERNON. That is exactly what things were originally made for.
— Oscar Wilde, "The Importance of Being Earnest"[3]

• • •

Attempts to "sound out" the work of Kay Rosen still do not result in a proclamation from either us or it. If they did, it would be far, far less. Instead, the speaking, reading, picturing and/or pronouncing of any of it (the "living with it") continues to provide multiple opportunities for a re(in)statement of the types of suggestive and expansive acts which started its visual and verbal enterprise in the first place. As I've written before, "one wonders how [Rosen] manages to construct façades that more than handle the sheer *overloading* of multiple interpretations instigated by her messages, without killing the messenger."4 Now I'm convinced that this or any other "assassination" will always be *refused* by what has remained (in the work's form and content) an assertion of nimble agility and not corrupting power. Challenging the oppression in the histories of both language and painting by deftly and succinctly utilizing many of what had been "The Master's Tools"5—formalism (shape, size, scale), humor (jokes, puns), linguistics (structural, comparative), psychoanalysis, semiotics, so on and so forth—Rosen has put together a truly *feminist* painting practice, defined constructively as such if you accept that term (as I do) as one which dramatically expands, rather than limits, the comprehensiveness of her work or anything else. Such an optimistic grasp becomes all the more meaningful—as in serious, critical and comical—when it comes from the body of painting itself, its strange, stone-still "remains" forever remaining out of the reach of death.6 With apologies to T.S. Eliot, in a "Rosen Room" all of the deaths of Painting come and go, provoking me to say—to quote the wonderfully terrible pun of an early work by the artist—"carry on, carrion."

The "eager promptitude" of Rosen's work (it is too perfect that this is the phrase I found when I looked up "alacrity" in my dictionary) does not change the fact that facing it in person usually leads to a thoroughly stubborn challenge, albeit a good-natured one. We join a tussle that is in the works themselves in a situation held in a special kind of cleverly oxymoronic "suspended animation." On one hand there is a meaningful, even poignant, *stillness*—not only of that embodied "in" the consistent structures of letter forms which spell out everyday words and phrases (a consistency shared by the relatively "concrete" architectural and social settings used in Rosen's work from the 1970s and early 1980s), but also of that situated "on" the causal condition of colorful, emphatic and flatly sign-painted surfaces and/or objects. On the other hand the work never relinquishes a critical, almost pulsing *liveliness*—a "continuous present" substantiating its presence in that never-ending (human) process of language being written, read and spoken, as well as paintings being produced and presented, not to mention (prior and new) connections being (re)created and *used* for their value. Use-value in art being what it is at the end of the twentieth century (in other words, "what is it?"), Rosen manages to remain focused upon the life-and-death promise of her work and its certain inclusiveness, rather than settling for a definitive statement or demand. In all of it, we are "the speaker waiting to be found." The value of the (self-)discovery that her work sets up is realized in its connection to our *other* relationships, especially those that exist during our "talks" with words, things and people, which we (re)negotiate and resolve (temporarily) if only to complicate and vacate them again—in other words, we find ourselves to get lost.

· · ·

Attempts to locate the artist herself in the work bring us very quickly to a 1992 painting called *Also Known as Kay*. Almost "red-rosen" in color, it reads "akak" in simple lower-case, sans-serif, dark brown letters. Coming from someone whose name can be summed up in a single letter of the alphabet (a core source of her work, most recently offered in her billboard *HI* from 1997-98, which reads "ABCDEFGHI"), this painting is so much more than a picturing/exposing of an alias—"Kay" a.k.a. "k." Full of visual and aural "noise" (is someone choking? or maybe it's a short burst of Roy Lichtensteinian machine gun fire), fraught with implications biographical or not (a more than irreconcilable work from twenty years earlier, *Katherine Was Katherized and Katharsized*, which reveals Rosen's early connections to artists such as Jasper Johns and Larry Rivers, merits mention here), and fomenting a funny singsong cadence ("a, k, a, k" chanted as if everything's "O.K."), the painting ultimately is typical of all of her production in the endless provisions it makes for meaningful association saturation.

And as if it weren't enough on its own, *Also Known as Kay* on occasion shows up in the lower left corner of *Corpus*, a "work" that exists only as a temporary installation when thirteen specific paintings, all from 1992, are brought "home" to be hung together in a tight grid on a wall. An "anatomy" fleshed out by an artist born in Corpus Christi, Texas, *Corpus* is an entire world (view), encapsulating many of the subjects and linguistic maneuvers that have occupied Rosen for some time. Done in the colors of the insides and outsides of human bodies, its "communal" arrangement displays some very particular body parts in *Sleeveless*, in which letters are moved next to each other in descending order of quantity to make an "arm" ("eeeesssllv"); as well as *Click* and *Bloodclot*, in which two letters in each have been moved so close together that we first read "dick" and "bloodot" (I think of these paintings as having had surgical operations, along with *Cut Out*, an idiosyncratic work for Rosen in that an "o" is changed into a "c" by way of a square having been cut away from the canvas). The mind and its tricks emerge in the number games of *Four or Five*, in which the choice goes Roman and almost turns lily-white ("ivorv"), and also in the cultural split personalities of *Dr. Freud* and *Mr. Dreamreader*, two characters made for each other and for this corpus, not only because they both have had their vowels removed, but also because they specifically provide a high level of psychosexual intrigue, muttering under their breaths "drfrd," and, even better, "mrdrmrdr" (more on murderers to follow). Space and time are played out in *Zone*, in which a "z" appears to be just passing through ("ozne"), and in *Turn*, in which a "t" and a "u" make an abrupt "utrn." Alas, there is no sun, but there is both *Full Moon* ("moom") and *Crescent Moon* ("mccn"). And, finally bringing us full circle, in *Corpus*'s upper right corner lies *Missing in Action*, a potential "erasure" of *Also Known as Kay*, where dots have disappeared from the "i"s in a word that easily could have just remained "Miami," but, with "I," "me" or "my," "I am," and "M.I.A." all hidden in plain view, it's much more. And again, no surprise that this painting is another *re*appearance, bringing us back to a "miami" visited by Rosen twenty years earlier in *The Virtue of Spaces*.

Location, location, location: we know it's everything, so much so that we're likely to be intrigued when we learn that Rosen has lived and worked in Gary, Indiana, since the late 1960s.[7] Staying local and going global before it became an art world topic of conversation, Rosen began her career as an artist working with what she knew—having studied French, Spanish, and linguistics, not art—and what was at hand near her new home in "The North"; not only places and things, but also people and, ultimately, their obstacles and achievements. Moving north from "The South," and then staying put in Gary for lifestyle and political reasons, Rosen has demonstrated just how productive participation in an international (art or not) discourse can be from anywhere we may find ourselves—of course it is not unimportant that she has been a key participant in nearby Chicago's art scene and its history.

Even Rosen's early 1972 works, which to some extent work with the "vocabularies" of the classics of modern art—assemblage and collage; Picasso and Dada, etc.— display the autonomy of what they "say" in a voice that distinguishes itself from the more contemporary source of pop art, in particular the work of Ed Ruscha, with which Rosen was relatively unfamiliar at the time.[8] By the end of the decade, Rosen had stopped working directly with letters, words, and phrases, having turned to the formal and structural visual "languages" she discovered and identified with in the art of the day: conceptual art, of course, but, more importantly, the systematic performative endeavors of composer Steve Reich and dancers Trisha

IT IS AS POSSIBLE TO GO DOWN WITH ONE LINER AS WITH ANOTHER.

Did you hear the one about the chorus that began to go down?
The altos took to the life boats, leaving the basses to sync or swim.
That reminds me of the man who thought he was buying a can of tuna. (canned laughter)
When he opened it up, he found a bass instead. (canned laughter)
Wanna know how he knew it wasn't an alto?
He knew he hadn't bought Chicken of the Sea.

Brown and Lucinda Childs. The interplay between what are graphic and notational systems and physical movement in their work, not to mention a willingness to appropriate phrases and forms from popular culture, was surely more fully contextualized for Rosen by her viewing of the major Marcel Duchamp retrospective that traveled to The Art Institute of Chicago in March 1974.[9] Three years later, Rosen would exhibit a clear and hilarious homage: *Brides and Slinkies Descending the Staircase* (1977), a set of fifteen photographs (alternating static pictures of brides and Slinkies moving down stairs) installed as a tautological descension of the staircase at Moming Dance Center, a church-turned-performance-space in Chicago.

In the early 1980s, Rosen continued her implicitly textual and explicitly photographic investigations of structural systems and/or objects that "conduct" (in both senses of the word) movement, utilizing the "public space" of theater seats (*Changing Seats* of 1978), urban parks (*Gateway Park, Gary, Indiana II*, and *Hyde Park, Chicago, Illinois II*, both of 1980), and even political discourse (the very funny *A Song and Dance* of 1978, which juxtaposes the toe shoes of a ballerina with lines of text beginning with a malapropism from Chicago Mayor Richard J. Daley: "Together we must rise to ever higher and higher platitudes." Rosen screws up his screw-up in painstaking line-by-line fashion, ending with "Together we must rise like a hair-raising blunder from a malaprop character.") It is important to acknowledge that Rosen's work from this period never in the least leaves language behind; in fact, it exists first as actual written words or paths inscribed in pencil on paper, then as implication in the relational aspects of all of her friends and colleagues (including her husband Bud) who performed for the work and, once again, as it becomes action in us.

In 1980 Rosen started to "walk" back to language in a series of *Stairwalking* notations and diagrams that recorded the simultaneous passage of hypothetical walkers on staircases at the School of The Art Institute of Chicago, The Clocktower in New York, and the Museum of Contemporary Art in Chicago in different ways: "Directions/Rhythms," "Directions/Patterns," "By Fives," "Side by Side," "Up And Down." From their increased complexity emerged the "look" of a written language, scribed in ink and/or colored pencil, or even colored graphic tape on matte mylar, together with the physical and conceptual value of the paper as a *page*. Such a transformation quickly led to the watershed moment of her first artist book, *Lines on Lines* from 1982 (Fig. 1), which utilized strips of type set on a headliner machine that she

Figure 1 (left)
Kay Rosen
Lines on Lines, 1982 (detail)
artist's book
8 x 10 inches

Figure 2 (right)
Kay Rosen
A Niche, 1997
wall painting
installation view,
M.I.T. List Visual Arts Center

remembers as a "dinosaur" (in a Duchampian chocolate grinder sort of way). Finding a way to have her text and eat it too (i.e. actually write and use it), Rosen constructed the book using blue linear patterns on clear mylar overlays as a way to "comment" on blocks of black text on paper. Moreover, the book provided Rosen an opportunity to bring the specifics of her linguistic training directly into her art practice; it is full of very funny jokes (my favorite: "IT IS AS POSSIBLE TO GO DOWN WITH ONE LINER AS WITH ANOTHER.") and such facts as "The initial 'p' sound, a labial, carries with it a puff of air which is articulated through the lips with considerable force. The initial 'h' sound, a slit fricative or spirant, squeezes out an air column through the soft palate and back of the tongue in a relaxed and unforced manner." Of course, such information is given to suggest then that "Had the wolf *p*uffed and puffed rather than *h*uffed and puffed, he might have succeeded in blowing down the third pig's house." Word play to the extreme, *Lines on Lines* continues to provide Rosen food for thought, sustenance that in its essence is *civic*.

· · ·

> Too many exceptions, too many historical, ideological, and formal
> circumstances, implicate the text in actuality, even if a text may also be
> considered a silent printed object with its own unheard melodies. The
> concert of forces by which a text is engendered and maintained as a fact not
> of mute ideality but of *production* dispels the symmetry of even rhetorical
> oppositions.
>
> — Edward Said, "The World, the Text, and the Critic"[10]

Due at least in part to a growing irritation with the Reagan years, in 1983 Rosen turned up the heat that had been in her work all along and entered an amazingly productive period in her development, which by the end of the decade would substantiate her as one of the more important artists working with language at that time.[11] Confronting oppression head on, Rosen was also gradually moving herself back home to painting, demonstrating that its presence in her work should be understood as having personal political significance. On the way, she ignited a fuse with the structural, physical and ideological shock of *No Noose Is Good Noose* (1983). Derived and extended from what was to be a foldout in an unpublished artist book called *Mined*, its original graphic black-and-white "page-ness" has been recast as a *mise en scène* made from home improvement materials: masonite, plexiglass, and paint. (A new version of the page has been realized for this catalogue.) In its lean-to yet highly organized, time-based sprawl, stick figures label "revolutions" in circular terms ("partial," "complete," "counter") while being subjected to holes, loops, nooses, and a "whollop" (or "wholeloop"). "Some revolutions lead to advances. Rolling heads quite accidentally gave rise to the wheel," is the chilling report. At stage right, one figure is either escaping or headed by way of pushcart to a different death. Thoroughly stark and chock-a-block (yet somehow not without humor), *No Noose* literally stands out in Rosen's production as a transitional moment in which she directed the work back to painting not to retreat to an unexamined place of "pure" aesthetics, but rather to up the ante again.

Queasy realizations of the nation-state's capacity for abuse jump around like a twisted "Jeopardy" game in a series of small paintings on board from 1984-85, which can exist on occasion (like a certain amount of her overall production) as very large wall paintings (Fig. 2).[12] "I HAVE A SYNCHING FEELING THAT A LYNCHING IS OCCURRING," repeats *Sinking Feeling* twice in black on red. "A BIG STICK WITH A LOUD BARK IS A BOUGH WOUGH," boasts *Take a*

Bough. "THE BLAHND [LEADING] THE BLAHND," fingers *Alabama* in its depiction of blind stick figures holding red canes. And "MUM" is the Word in *Read Lips*, succinctly depicting the strength that can be found in (feminist) refusal, a position which also lurks just below the surface of one of Rosen's most to-the-point wall paintings, *Big Talk* (1985), which says "JUMBO MUMBO." The deeper implications of these works (obfuscation, even censorship) would be picked up again in 1990, in a series of "blocked out" paintings including *Little Statuette*, *You Lie Through Your Teeth*, and, most "complete," *Odd/Even*, which looks as if all of the letters that "should" be there have been covered up. In a text published for an exhibition of works from this period, Rosen submits that "In the absence of a linguistic system, meaning appears to be thwarted and blocked, but the pieces actually attempt to function as re-signifiers of meaning rather than as de-signifiers."[13] A major work from the same year takes a similar stance: the nearly "natural" wall painting, *The Forest for the Trees*, in which, if we look hard, we see that the letters of the phrase "for the trees" actually can be found in "the forest," but only by making it virtually impossible to see "the forest for the trees."

Back inside, it's no accident that *Jarred*, a small red painting from 1986, lives to this day in Rosen's kitchen. It's at home there not only because of its double depiction of a jarred jar ("JAR," "RED"), but also because it's the first thing you see when you come into the house from the garage. Related to several paintings and works on photocopies that played very "clipped" texts off of stylized gestural linear images (including *Bam, Boo* of 1985 and *Classic Pairs II*, *Loin/Proche*, and *The Mexican Revolution*, all of 1986), *Jarred* is significant likewise because it introduces a format that Rosen would adapt for several key paintings of the following year, the so-called "stacked" paintings, which employ multiple canvases to give the work more body (implying in addition that there could be things hidden between their layers) as well as added areas of contrasting color. The paradoxically graceful cobbling together of these paintings heightens the virility of their suggestiveness—all of these "male-identified" paintings receive a personality adjustment, leaving us unsure if any are what they seem. *Edgar Degas* goes (of all things) Brooklyn and becomes "ED ga/de GA"; *Mr. Ed, Missed* loses some unknown opportunity but does catch a glimpse of his "feminine side"; *No, Noah, Ah, Noah* seems not to know *what* to do; and *Go on, Goon* is self-explanatory. Living with their various "facial" tics, these paintings are *alive* if only because they're clearly quite annoyed.

Jump forward for a moment to a painting like *Partners* (1991), in which "TOM CAN CHA," or "TOM TOM, CAN CAN, CHA CHA" ("canya or canchya?" is the question here), and Rosen's dance card remains—euphemistically speaking—fraught with possibilities. Returning to *John Wilkes Booth* (1987), which breaks the murderer into bits ("ass ass/in in/the the/ater")[14], we are advised that, yes, acts of violence and brutal assertions of power usually result in death, but in Rosen's case it is a "stilling" of particular pictures by rapid-fire accruals of quick-witted interpretations (in other words, agility, not power). Witness the drama of *The "Ed" Paintings* (1988), in which, as Judith Russi Kirshner put it, "Rosen has expanded on the one-liner to create dramas that look like signs but tell stories, complete with action, suspense, murder, a hero named Ed, and some of the shortest plots ever shown."[15] The lowly, rather defenseless suffix "-ed" (it puts things in the past tense, it is thoroughly inactive) becomes "Ed" only to suffer a terrible fate at the hands of a strangely rigorous lack of clarity (what are the roles of "Rosa" and "Blanch"?), not to mention the doubly emasculating indignation of a dead "Mike" (as in microphone), a detail made poignant by the final action implied in the last painting of the series, *Ex-ed*, in which a distinctly red "memory" is "erased" by an obfuscating "X." Before we jump to reactionary conclusions (those sexist ones that assume any feminist assertion is by definition

"TODAY" Series   The Date Paintings of 1967   October 27 to December 4, 1977   Otis Art Institute Gallery   2401 Wilshire Boulevard   Los Angeles, California 90057

Figure 3 (left)
Poster for
"On Kawara 1967" exhibition
Otis Art Institute Gallery
October 27-December 4, 1977

Figure 4 (right)
Mary Heilmann
My Heart Is a Flower, 1992
oil on canvas
two panels, overall 71 x 61 inches
Courtesy Pat Hearn Gallery,
New York

"hysterical"), Rosen asks us to bear in mind the truth of a "calm" painting like *Six* (1988): "tworkov, twombly, twomen," it mentions in passing, reminding us how often some of us are entitled to as much as double of almost anything. Rosen continues to keep the jury out: on the one hand there is a painting like *Tide* of 1994 ("sirf girls, serf gerls, surf gurls," the "waves" of feminism cascading in a dagger-like font); on the other a work like *Crotchety* (1997), in which the word precariously dangles you know where.

• • •

Bringing things "back to life" again, I'll jump to some of the paintings from 1993—*Deaf, Double Whammy, Little Sheep, Still Life,* and *Trickknees*—examples from a group that share the typeface Futura Bold and a significant move into a newly expanded range of vibrant, straight-from-the-can colors. The words in these paintings either do or do not contain letterforms that are superfluous linguistically speaking—meaning you don't need them to pronounce the word "correctly." If this is true, then their purpose could be "purely" pictorial, ripe for a painting situation where color takes precedence. Earlier, in a major piece called *Untitled Grid* (1990), Rosen ran a full spectrum of referents—many of them alphabetical—through the color wheel, resulting in everything from a rusty Volkswagen ("rstuvw"), to the opposite of a famous Italian painter ("antititian"), to the middle of a film noir ("lmno"). Turning the tables, she then went on to produce a series of "silver" paintings in 1991 that took advantage of the reflective, color-restricted nature of their surfaces to act out the implications of balance, equilibration, and mirroring in binary words and phrases: *Tidbit, Divide, Inez Has One Nose,* etc. While recalling to some extent the informational status of institutional signage, many of them are among Rosen's most playful paintings: *Stunts,* in particular, is an acrobat that shows the word either flipped over "flat" on its back or in the process of bench-pressing its weight on two "t"s.

Color and language are always a tricky pair, if only because descriptions always fail (do I see what you see?). The vibrant colors of the 1993 paintings energize that "liveliness" mentioned above, a "way of life" that, at least for paintings, cheats death. In this regard, the work of On Kawara (Fig. 3) is a crucial precedent, with his "locational" approach to painting and subject matter that can never be anything but the everyday. As Lucy Lippard rightfully claimed in her 1977 catalogue essay for "On Kawara 1967," an exhibition of the artist's series of "Today" paintings at the [then] Otis Art Institute Gallery in Los Angeles: "Perhaps the most important aspect of making the date paintings is the eight or nine hours it takes to make one. The letters and numbers are not stenciled, but painted with infinite patience and visual exactitude. Kawara's medium is not paint and brush so much as it is Slow Time."[16] As the artist well-known for his statement "I am still alive," Kawara also understands how much of that slow existence depends upon color; Rosen, despite the misleading name of the "One-Shot" sign paint she uses, feels and works the same deliberate way as Kawara does, and manages to take advantage of the relative "speeds" of color as one way in which to turn the work away from herself and toward us. To that end, I believe Rosen's closest contemporary is Mary Heilmann (Fig. 4), who in her use of color and abstraction as vernacular languages also takes more than enough time to provide beautifully for the "life" of the work, not to mention those of the "speakers to be found."

Nowhere is this life-span more present than in *Still Life*, a bright yellow canvas on which rest the raspberry-colored words "FRUIT DISH," topped with extra cherrylike dots over the capital "I"s. I took this painting very personally in 1994 as one that asks "Who among us—*any* of us—has not known a still life, a life no longer moving, a nature morte too soon?"[17] Given the times, of course, I had on my mind then (as did the artist) such things as the AIDS crisis—which we haven't forgotten—but it is important to acknowledge that the painting tells us just as resolutely that it is in fact *still* life, not (yet) death. Rosen had addressed the AIDS crisis directly in 1990 with a project for Art Against AIDS, producing a bus placard in which synonyms for the word "aids"—assistance, help, support, etc.—overcome the brutality of the acronym by standing in line in a block of pink. Moreover, *Still Life* and the rest of the 1993 paintings have as their counterpart the black-and-white wall painting, *Phantom Limb* (1993/96), which has been described as follows by the artist:

> Audially, "p" and "b" are phantom letters and don't exist at all. The sensation of "feeling" in this amputated limb comes only through the *visual* presence of the two letters. Oddly enough, the lower case "p" is the same letter form as the "b," turned upside down. Together they seem to represent a single neurological sensation which travels from one end of the limb to the other, where it reverses course and then travels back in the opposite direction.[18]

The body of Rosen's work, then, remains complex, fluid, in between, sometimes androgynous, transsexual—from *Directions for a Man-Lady* of 1972 (done in response to a game she played with her young son, who would place the black piece of Chuckles candy as if it were a mustache between her nose and mouth), to *Mr. Ed, Missed*, to *Georgy, Porgy, Bess* (where Porgy doesn't have to make any choice), to a blunt wall painting from 1996 called *She-Man* ("SHE, HE, HER" tumbling down its façade). In some ways, her most poignant works are those that use lists taken from places like the Gary telephone book (*Ugly Duckling* of 1990), the opus of Franz Liszt (*Liszt* of 1990), and the saga of "The Man Who Would Be King" (*The Man* of 1991, Fig. 5). Moreover, there is *Sisyphus* (1991)—a list of seventy-two misspellings of the doomed man's name that ends with "sissyfuss"—which exists as a blue satin ribbon, and is performed in a stand-up-comedy-style video in which each misnomer is accompanied by a drum roll and a rim shot. Even when they're embarrassing and laughable, it never becomes a cliché to suggest that these lists *are* life, moments that account for who and where we are in the world, and what we did while we were here.

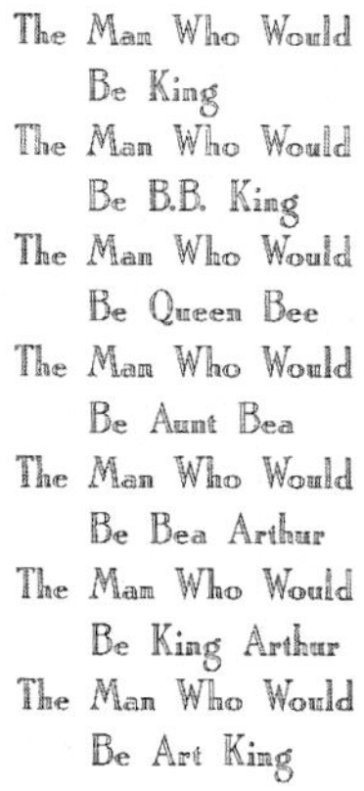

The Man Who Would
   Be King
The Man Who Would
   Be B.B. King
The Man Who Would
   Be Queen Bee
The Man Who Would
   Be Aunt Bea
The Man Who Would
   Be Bea Arthur
The Man Who Would
   Be King Arthur
The Man Who Would
   Be Art King

Figure 5
Kay Rosen
The Man, 1991
etching, edition of 32
25.5 x 19.5 inches

Borrowing again from Scott Long's "The Loneliness of Camp," I find myself *proclaiming* that "[t]his essay is a defense of camp as a moral activity. It is predicated in part on the idea that terms such as *moral* are more and more being vitiated and stripped of meaning in our society. Hence to use this term here, as though I am somehow privileged to speak it or invest it with force, may seem a contradiction in terms."[19] The composite body of all of Rosen's work is by nature *camp*, particularly as it materializes the essence of Long's newly capable version of the descriptive term, which he (among others) had retrieved from trivialization: "The unity the observer finds [in camp] is not the formal unity bourgeois criticism seeks (a camp aesthetic necessarily mocks formalism, does not respect the separation between the art object and the 'real' world of content and contradiction): it is a different unity, dialectical in that it emerges from a conflict of values."[20] For Rosen, and for us, this conflict of values remains—with firm resolve, good humor, and liberatory significance—a viable matter of life and death.[21]

Notes

1. Gertrude Stein, "Composition as Explanation," originally published in 1926, as reprinted in *Selected Writings of Gertrude Stein* (New York: Vintage Books, 1990), 521-22.

2. Scott Long, "The Loneliness of Camp," originally published as "Useful Laughter: Camp and Seriousness," in *Southwest Review* 74 (Winter 1989), as reprinted in David Bergman, ed., *Camp Grounds: Style and Homosexuality* (Amherst: University of Massachusetts Press, 1993), 84.

3. Oscar Wilde, "The Importance of Being Earnest," originally produced in 1895, as reprinted in Richard Ellmann, ed., *The Picture of Dorian Gray and Other Writings by Oscar Wilde* (New York: Bantam Books, 1982), 417.

4. Terry R. Myers, "Kay Rosen," *Arts Magazine* 66 (April 1992): 75.

5. See Audre Lorde, "The Master's Tools Will Never Dismantle the Master's House," first given as comments at "The Personal and the Political Panel," Second Sex Conference, New York, September 29, 1979, as reprinted in *Sister Outsider: Essays & Speeches by Audre Lorde* (Freedom, Calif.: The Crossing Press, 1984). In another essay included in the volume—"Poetry Is Not a Luxury," from 1977—Lorde hits the nail on the head when she reminds women that "within living structures defined by profit, by linear power, by institutional dehumanization, our feelings were not meant to survive." (p. 39)

6. I attempt another analysis of the relationship between contemporary painting and its "perpetual" deaths in my essay "Jumping the gun, better than dead: what's next in Peter Doig's paintings," in *Peter Doig Blizzard seventy-seven*, exh. cat. (Kiel: Kunsthalle zu Kiel; Nürnberg: Kunsthalle Nürnberg; and London: Whitechapel Art Gallery, 1998), 65-72.

7. Rosen herself has provided the best accounting of her life working in Gary, Indiana, worth citing in its entirety:

    Sometimes I feel like a black sheep when I say I am from Gary. People always ask, "Ewe live in Gary?" No one ever asks, "Do ewe graze in Gary?" Or, "Is the grass greener in Gary?" They do ask, "Do bullets graze in Gary?" Bullets, like diplomats, explorers and elks, lodge everywhere. Did Henry Cabot lodge in Gary? I doubt it. Neither did John Cabot nor Sebastian Cabot. Father Jacques Marquette, a French explorer, did lodge here temporarily. A nearby school, church and park are named after him; and his statue in the park attests to that fact. Art in the parque in Guerrey. The French influence is minimal, though. My work was somewhat minimal for awhile, but I do not think there is any connection between the two. Connections are hard to nail down if they are not tangible. I guess that is why there is a monument to Father Marquette—to establish a concrete connection with the past. I do not know whether or not the statue is concrete; but I *do* know it has not weathered because it is spray-painted a copperish bronze color, and the paint has not cracked, faded or peeled over the years.

    Written as an artist statement for the catalogue of "Indiana Influence," an exhibition at the Fort Wayne Museum of Art in 1984, this text also hits home for me, given its publication in my Indiana hometown. Such beginnings, of course, give me little interest (it's really a bias) in overdetermining the meaning of making contemporary art in Gary (not that the city isn't interesting, even provocative: The Jackson Five, the second black mayor in the U.S., and a lengthy tradition of radicalized politics and union stuff). The artist herself shares this disinterest, even though when given the opportunity, she'll enjoy the irony—consider, for example, her 1995 exhibition at the Indianapolis Museum of Art, which she smartly called "Back Home in Indiana," dropping the "again" in the famous song's title. For a good "outsider" take on the Indiana situation, and an "insider" take on the crucially important Jewish question in Rosen's work, see Rhonda Lieberman, "Recent Painting by Jewish Woman in Indiana," *Art + Text*, no. 46 (September 1993): 54-59.

8. The relationship between Rosen's and Ruscha's work is self-evident, although it seems to cut both ways—one wonders if some of Rosen's later works (in particular the paintings from 1990 in which some text has been blocked out) were in fact a recent influence on, for example, his "Cityscape" paintings from 1994 to 1997 [see Edward Ruscha, *Cityscapes/O Poetry*, exh. cat. (New York: Leo Castelli Gallery, 1997)]. With that in mind, Yve Alain-Bois's essay for an exhibition of Ruscha's "Liquid" paintings brilliantly outlines the pop artist's relationship to "visual noise," focusing on that gap between what we see and what we say that also informs Rosen's work: "In fact, it is just this lack of coincidence between two linguistic codes (spoken sounds of language, written words) that gives us a clue as to what Ruscha means by 'visual noise': something surreptitiously lost in the alphabetical transcription, and it is the peculiar quality of what is lost to any kind of daily perception (that is, not necessarily linguistic ones) that seems to be at the core of Ruscha's art." Yve Alain-Bois, "Thermometers Should Last Forever," in *Edward Ruscha: Romance With Liquids. Paintings 1966-1969*, exh. cat. (New York: Gagosian Gallery and Rizzoli, 1993), 12. I would submit that Rosen is constantly aware of the necessity and value of the everyday in her work, recapturing it in the double entendre of a situation that is essentially *domestic* without reverting to the old sexist trap of that word.

9. See Anne d'Harnoncourt and Kynaston McShine, eds., *Marcel Duchamp*, exh. cat. (New York: The Museum of Modern Art; and Philadelphia: Philadelphia Museum of Art, 1973). Included in this catalogue is a treasure trove of essays applicable to Rosen's work, most particularly Michel Sanouillet's "Marcel Duchamp and the French Intellectual Tradition" and David Antin's "Duchamp and Language."

10. Edward Said, "The World, the Text, and the Critic," in *The World, the Text, and the Critic* (Cambridge, Mass.: Harvard University Press, 1983), 49-50. In this essay, Said invokes the fascinating and, for my purposes, germane story of "a remarkably sophisticated and unexpectedly prophetic school of [eleventh-century] Islamic philosophic grammarians, whose polemics anticipate twentieth-century debates between structuralists and generative grammarians, between descriptivists

and behaviorists." He continues: "Batinists held that meaning in language is concealed within the words; meaning is therefore available only as the result of an inward-tending exegesis. The Zahirites—their name derives from the Arabic word for clear, apparent, and phenomenal; *Batin* connotes internal—argued that words had only a surface meaning, one that was anchored to a particular usage, circumstance, historical and religious situation." (p. 36)

11. It is, of course, not a mistake to discuss Rosen's work in relation to that of Jenny Holzer and Barbara Kruger, among many others. Doing so, however, one should remember what Tim Porges noticed in Rosen's work: "This is not the second-person direct speech favored by Holzer or Kruger. There's no increase or problematization of intimacy, no erosion of distance. The voice is third-person throughout; cheerful, impersonal, affectless. It's hardly a voice at all, really, except for the occasional hint of a southern accent." Tim Porges, "Kay Rosen," *New Art Examiner 22* (November 1994): 39. I would add once again that one key reason there seems to be "hardly a voice" is that Rosen's work patiently waits for *ours*.

12. The use of the wall as a literal support for some of Rosen's paintings maintains her requirement that the work directly vitalize structural social space. With the walls it is usually given rather than created. Two distinct examples are *Leak* (1995), in which "FLOOR" is painted right-side up next to its namesake, while "ROOF" is upside-down at the top of the wall with a gap between its second "O" and the "F"—a "missing" "L" having "leaked" onto the "floor"; and *A Niche* (1997), in which "A NI"/"ETZS"/"CHE" is distributed across its three walls, effectively breaking a (super)man, if you will, putting him in his place.

13. *Little Critic Pamphlet Three: Kay Rosen, paintings 1990* (London: Victoria Miro Gallery, 1990).

14. It's possible that it was this implicit violence, as well as the ways in which *John Wilkes Booth* displayed its broken text (along with other paintings from the same body of work, including *Dred Scott* and *Wild Blue Yonder*), that struck Christopher Wool when he first saw these paintings in Rosen's February 1988 exhibition at Feature, while he was in Chicago for a presentation on the work of Dieter Roth given at the gallery. According to Ann Goldstein, Wool began his "word" paintings in 1987; living in New York then, I recall that the "broken" ones emerged the following year. See Ann Goldstein, "What They're Not: The Paintings of Christopher Wool," in *Christopher Wool*, exh. cat. (Los Angeles: The Museum of Contemporary Art; and Zurich: Scalo Verlag, 1998), 255-64.

15. Judith Russi Kirshner, "read read rosens," *Artforum 29* (December 1990): 94. See Connie Butler's essay in this catalogue for Rosen's own synopsis of these paintings.

16. Lucy R. Lippard, "Just in Time: On Kawara," in *On Kawara 1967*, exh. cat. (Los Angeles: Otis Art Institute Gallery, 1977), n.p. I consider Rosen's show to be a reasserting of all that surely had been mentally and physically tangible in Kawara's work during its "life" in the day-to-day activity of an art school.

17. Terry R. Myers, "Kay Rosen," *Blocnotes*, no. 5 (Winter 1994): 69. Translated into French.

18. Kay Rosen, "LIFELI|K|E," forthcoming in Stanley Tigerman, ed., *Archeworks: Morality and Ethics* (New York: The Monacelli Press, 1999).

19. Long, 78.

20. Ibid, 89.

21. This essay would not exist without the valuable conversations I've had over several years with Linda Burnham, Laura Cottingham, Linda Daniels, Tavia Fortt, Vanessa Jackson, Jonathan Katz, Larry Johnson, Jill Levine, Sue Spaid, and, of course most importantly, Kay Rosen.

(B)ecoming (A)part

A project by Kay Rosen for

du: Die Zeitschrift der Kultur, Zurich, 1993

Linguistic systems are a consensus of rules which are products of history and usage. This consensus functions in an active and passive capacity: delivering information (speaking and writing) and receiving it (hearing and reading). Because language is an abstract system of signs and symbols, and because context is variable, interpretation is subjective. But there remains broad and mutual agreement on the significance and function of such primary components of (Indo-European) language and grammar as letters and spaces. In the micro space of words and short phrases the function of these fundamental elements is more critical to constructing meaning than in longer passages. The interest of the work lies here, where the absence, presence, rearrangement, or alteration of these small units disturbs linguistic sequence, revealing patterns and systems which exceed and outperform their expected function.

Lesson 1 recounts a very economical and succinct little tale from only three words, exhorting its nine letters to create drama from a verb, a conjunction, and a noun. The letter A, followed by two D's, spells ADD. As if the spelling were implementing the meaning, the D's indeed increase or accumulate. In addition, the replacement of the middle D with N, to create the word AND, obeys the directive of ADD by supplementing it with another word. The new word, AND, also satisfies its own definition as a connective, joining word by its position between two words. Substituting E for A, to create the final word END, completes the sequence. The meaning of each word complies with its chronological position. A minimal, almost subliminal, operation of displacing one letter in each word, allows ADD to systematically transform itself into a brief generic narrative, generating a middle and end out of its simple, unspectacular origin. Reading must be active and discerning to distinguish the rudiments of a story in this very condensed text.

Alternative systems of investigating and analyzing language, like my project, sometimes require alternative systems of reading. When a word is restructured non-linearly, normal methods of decoding (reading) are not sufficient. How does one read **TRICKKNEES** written like this, with the KK's dislocated on the middle line, similar to the position of the knee cap on the leg? What is the significance of this conspicuous realignment, besides its attempted sumilation of the body? And what might the slight separation of the components of K suggest?

Lesson 2: **TRICKKNEES** can be pronounced the same way without the K's—**TRICNEES**. The K's are excessive letters which can be released from any phonetic function to serve as independent agents in a pictorial capacity, like little stick legs. Although the two pairs are in synch with each other, like little dancers, each pair has one "leg" which is awkwardly and unnaturally bent, like the one in the expression of the same name describing a flawed knee which goes out of joint from time to time. Demonstrating their physical capabilities here, the K's act as surrogates or assistants to meaning, helping to convey the sense of the word by single-handedly performing it. The meaning of **TRICKKNEES** is unofficially about the accidental and coincidental intersection of such formal elements as letter forms with meaning. Because of the convergence of structure and meaning, one might actually come close to understanding the concept of **TRICKKNEES** merely by observing the K's, without reconstructing the entire word linguistically.

TRIC
KK
NEES

In a depleted and stratified arrangement of C's, A's, and T's, the thought of cats might come to mind. But the absence of letters is as important as their presence. One must consider the reason for the intervals. There is a rigorous and efficient logic in all of the work; the choices are not arbitrary. So it is probable that this sparse collection of letters is about something other than cats.

Lesson 3: It is odd that STACCATO, a word which concerns intervals of silence between musical notes, contains three pairs of letters, each of which is separated by various intervals of space (other letters). It is not really necessary for the reader to play the game, "Guess the Word"; although I would be very impressed by someone who figured out that this word was STACCATO without having read the title. Rather, it interests me more to pass on this new information about STACCATO to the reader: that the formal structure of its letters and its meaning are parallel. This occurrence is not a function of formal rules, but an independent event in which letters double as musical notes of different time values. In order to reconstruct meaning, the reader is invited to become a viewer, to see and to reason rather than to read, that the C's, A's, and T's and their intermittent symmetrical positions in the word are more aligned with tempo and musical considerations than with linguistic ones. This structural complement to the meaning of STACCATO serves as an extra-linguistic spine or armature which may be invisible in complete, linear words, but which, when isolated and exposed, inadvertently confirms and reinforces meaning. There seems to me to be something very ethical about a word which can offer this sort of structural evidence to support its meaning, and visually validate and corroborate its conceptual intent.

Lesson 4: This stack of fragments looks like exclamations from a comic strip—something between OUCH and UGH—partial and inarticulate expressions of disgust or pain. But their neat, clean-cut margins make them appear to have been surgically, aesthetically, and conceptually removed from larger words. Without the rest, one can only speculate about what they mean or how they sound. It is a very literal attempt to show how critical context is to meaning. Not only is the surrounding text important, but so is the larger context: historical, cultural, political, the medium, the voice of the author, the identity of the audience. All contribute to and impact on meaning, organically shaping and manipulating it, but never allowing it to harden and dry. When reinserted into the three words ROUGHLY THOUGHT THROUGH, the fragments become semantically distinct and phonetically coherent. They react to the letters which precede and follow, changing their vowel sounds from U (ruffly) to O (thot) to OO (THROO). When activated by adjacent letters, the phrase can be read normally. Otherwise it can only be addressed in terms of deficiency. Yet deficiency is the message of the phrase. Information is never complete. There always remain elusive and inaccessible ingredients outside of one's field of knowledge which prevent complete comprehension. In a reduced and partial context, ideas are incapable of being tho*roughly* thought through.

Reading numbers such as 9 and 6 is indisputable until they are considered along with the upside down word NEIN. Maybe the numbers are inverted as well and should be 6 and 9? Nevertheless, the phrase indicates a need for correction, both in the "answers" and in the vertical orientation of the word. If the page is turned, so that NEIN reads right side up, our and its position are reconciled visually; and we feel comfortable with our mutual alignment. But this solution corrects only the orientation system of the page, not the number sequence. They remain the same wrong and right answers, 9 and 6; and the rest of the magazine is out of whack. If only the text (and not the page) is mentally inverted to read 6 NEIN 9, the orientation of NEIN is resolved, and the magazine is in tact. But the new numbers are still "incorrect"; we are still told NEIN. To confound this binary ambiguity even more, consider the word NEIN, which means NO in this form, but sounds and looks like a slightly rearranged version of the English number NINE (9). Is it possible that this is not an issue of translation, orientation, or arithmetic after all, but simply an incident of mispelling, which should read instead 9 NINE 6 (996) or 6 NINE 9 (699)?

Lesson 5: Function and position in relation to a system are complex and uneasy. Criteria and methods of orientation are conditional. Complete agreement and accommodation are unlikely.

Lesson 6: A background in languages, comparative linguistic analysis, and applied linguistics provides a rigorous method and discipline for scrutinizing language, for focusing on the smallest mechanisms by which it operates, and for dissecting and analyzing almost invisible components of language. But academia does not furnish a sympathetic framework or audience for investigating and presenting alternative ideas which come from digging around in language and excavating unnoticed sub-systems which operate independently of authorized rules. Nor does it seem to be entertained by linguistic events which are odd or funny because of the rules. Because many of these unintentional sub-systems and events are revealed and understood through seeing, it is useful, but incompatible with that system, to present this information visually, through painting, drawing, or the visual page. It is remarkable how written information can also be processed through deductions and associations, relying very little on the learned, cognitive process of reading. Visual strategies of grammar and typography such as spacing, upper and lower case, punctuation, type size and boldness, letter forms, and layout are critical to interpretation, but improper academic issues. They can contribute significantly to the way information is received, as can such concerns of art as color, surface, composition, scale. They may not have much to do with linguistic structure; but they are capable of structuring meaning visually, through emphasis or de-emphasis, for example. They function as much like signs and directives for reading as do phonemes. But they are not even a blip on the screen of the academic study and teaching of languages. An alternative to changing the system, working uneasily within it, or leaving it entirely was to combine the paradigm of the classroom or "laboratory" with that of the studio, inventing a hybrid from elements of both.

RAG
GED
EDG E
E DGE

It is improbable that one belongs to a singular system. And within the larger category of Art, there are clearly multiple subdivisions. Where an artist fits is questionable and variable, whether it is her stated concern or not. Like many others, I have not intended to actively or consciously define an agenda or negotiate a position. Those classifications are often constructed externally by others from perceptions about artists and perceptions of trends and issues, for example: language in art, women in art, women who use language in art, women who claim authorship of language, women who teach, women who paint, gender as an issue in painting, small painting as a gender issue, medium as message, hidden messages, word as image, word as concept and image, the sign as page, the page as sign, the canvas as sign and page, unauthorized voices, art on the edge, art on the fringe, outsider art, alternative messages, humor in art, humor by women, humor in work by American women. All of these constructs can be used to define a (1) woman who (2) paints (usually) (3) small (usually) (4) images of language (mostly English), which because of their authorship, content, size, and process lie neither within historically validated categories of painting nor within historically validated categories of linguistics.

Lesson 7: If one reads this page diagonally from upper left to lower right (C-E-N) and upper right to lower left (T-E-R), she reads CENTER; and there appears to be one big E in the middle. But the movement of the eye makes an X. No, it suggests. There is not one center, but two. There is an E in the middle of each syllable. CENTER is plural.

Lesson 1 began with the work's intention of discovering and analyzing new visual and linguistic systems in brief verbal fragments. Because every mark that is made on a page creates meaning, shorter constructions generally provide stricter and more rigorous limits and controls on interpretation than do longer ones. This last lesson offers a very literal scenario on the polemics of size. The dispute concerns quantity—the sum of letters/numbers per line, nine or ten, which is indicated by the final number expressed on that line. For example, N-I-N-E-N-E-I-N-1-0 does indeed contain ten figures. Each line attempts to be specific, clear, and correct in its procedure and solution, enlisting a variety of strategies, such as reiteration, translation, and enumeration to make its case. But in spite of their insistence, the voice or voices contradict themselves and each other. Their disagreement is a consequence of expression. The subtraction or addition of each unit of meaning, each letter or number, increases or decreases the length of the argument and thus, the conclusion.

Lesson 8 is a farcical and elaborate conceit about the behavior of language and its inability to be absolute, certain, and consistent. Moreover, it demonstrates how critical the smallest components are to this behavior.

TEN NO NINE
NINE NEIN 10
10 NO NEIN 9
9 NO NEIN TEN
TEN NO NEIN

Plates

Carry On, Carrion, 1972
mixed media on paper
18 x 12 inches

Carry On, Carrion   Kay 9 Rosen September

Directions for a Man-Lady, 1972
mixed media on paper
18 x 12 inches

1 CHUCKLES

2. REMOVE
LICORICE
3. PUT BETWEEN
NOSE & MOUTH

Directions for a MAN-LADY   Kay G. Foren October 1972

Changing Seats, 1978
black-and-white photograph
60.5 x 45 inches

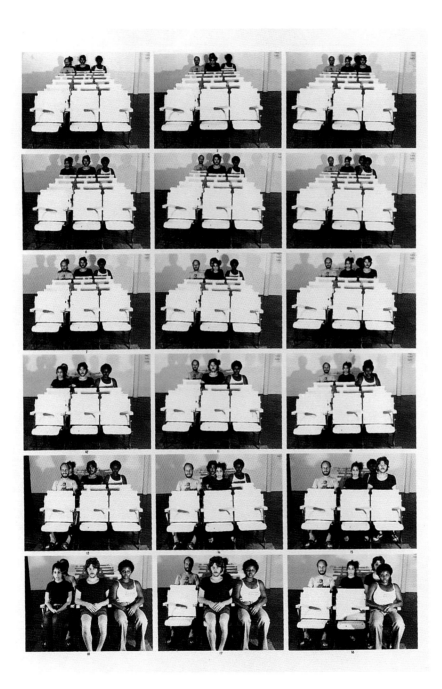

Gateway Park, Gary, Indiana II, 1980
photograph, ink, and china marker on paper
two panels, each 20 x 24 inches

Hyde Park, Chicago, Illinois II, 1980
photograph, ink, and china marker on paper
two panels, each 20 x 24 inches

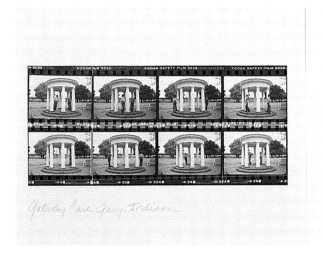

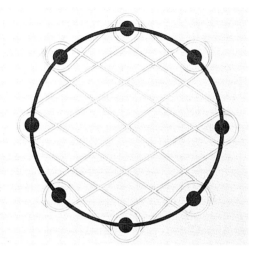

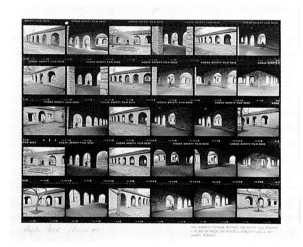

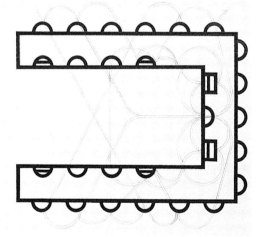

Stairwalking: Three Staircases, 1980
gelatin silver print
20 x 24 inches

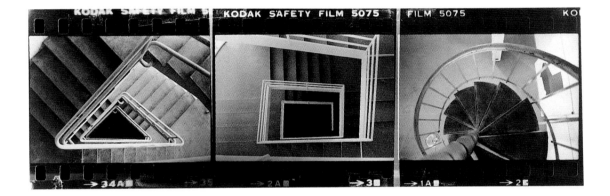

Stairwalking: Up and Down, 1981
India ink, colored pencil, and
black-and-white photograph on paper
23 x 14.5 inches

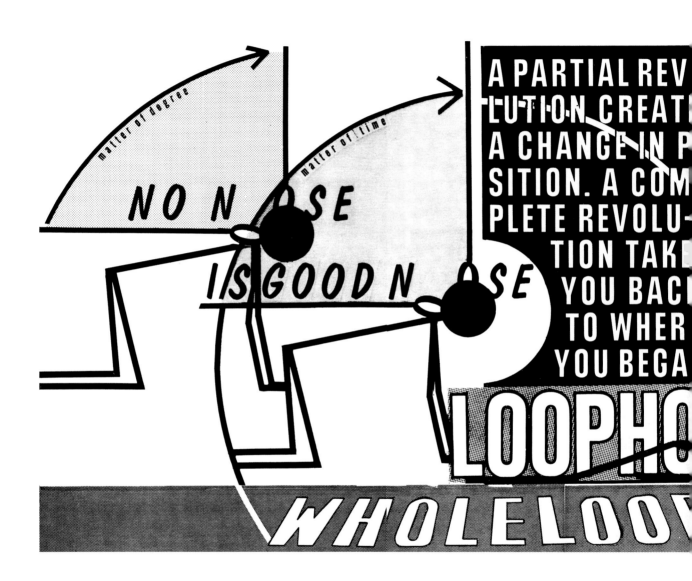

matter of degree

matter of time

NO N OSE

IS GOOD N OSE

A PARTIAL REV
LUTION CREAT
A CHANGE IN P
SITION. A COM
PLETE REVOLU
TION TAKE
YOU BAC
TO WHER
YOU BEGA

LOOPHO

WHOLELOO

Some revolutions lead to advances. Rolling heads quite accidentally gave rise to the wheel.

"YOU GO ON A HEAD. I WILL CATCH UP LATER."

Border Peece, 1984
installation view, Broadway Window,
The New Museum of Contemporary Art,
New York

Big Talk, 1985
billboard
part of a Group Material project sponsored by
Randolph Street Gallery, Chicago, 1990

Leroy Was Here, 1984
Sinking Feeling, 1984 (two panels)
Glamour, 1985
Skin Niks, 1984
Read Lips, 1984 (three panels)
Honk if You're Foul, 1984
Alabama, 1984 (two panels)
Eyesore, 1984
Blub, Blub, Blub, 1985 (three panels)
Take a Bough, 1984
sign paint on museum board
each panel 17 x 11 inches

VIVE LE ROI!
RAH, RAH
APRES MOI,
LE DELUGE
OH, EAU
COUP D'ETAT
TA, TA
LE ROI EST MORT
EH, MORT !

I HAVE A
SYNCHING
FEELING
THAT A
LYNCHING IS
OCCURRING

I HAVE A
SYNCHING
FEELING
THAT A
LYNCHING IS
OCCURRING

KNIGHTS
IN LOVE
NIGHTS
IN ARMOR

muy, muy

BACK
BITING
CALLS
FOR
BITING
BACK
yum-yum

M

M

U

U

M

M

QUACKS
DUCK

DOWN, DOWN!
FUZZ, FUZZ!

LEADING
THE BLAHND   THE BLAHND
Blahnds
May Not Have   Some Canes
More Fun But   Are Able
They Can Sure   Some Ain't
Try Dying   Some Cain And
                    Some Cain't

SORE SIGHT
FO(U)R EYES
Seeing Red
is the result of
the spectacles
you are wearing
or the spectacle
you are watching

BLUB   BLUB   BLUB

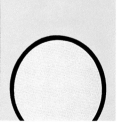
A BIG STICK
WITH A
LOUD BARK
IS A
BOUGH
WOUGH
When the bough breaks,
So does the wough
-UGH-UGH

The Mexican Revolution, 1986
sign paint on photocopy
24 x 37.5 inches

Edgar Degas, 1987
sign paint on canvas
two panels, each 10 x 10 x 2.75 inches

Go on, Goon, 1987
sign paint on canvas
four panels, each 10 x 10 x 2 inches

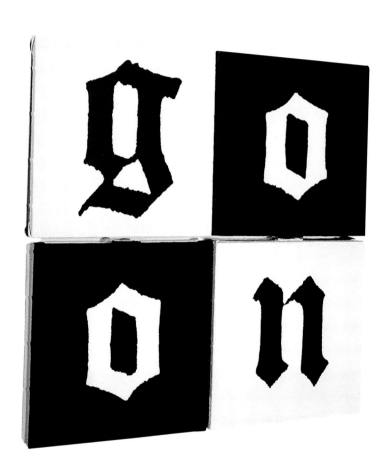

Mr. Ed, Missed, 1987
sign paint on canvas
10 x 20 x 2.75 inches

John Wilkes Booth, 1987
sign paint on canvas
20 x 20 inches

tworkov
twombly
twomen

The "Ed" Paintings (Surprise; Technical Difficulties;
Sp-spit it Out; Blanks [two panels]; *Ex-ed),* 1988
sign paint on canvas
six panels, each 32 x 20 inches

TREE
LINED
TREE

Oh, Eau, 1989/92
installation view (including *Same*, 1992),
Laura Carpenter Gallery, Santa Fe, 1992

Little Statuette, 1990
sign paint on canvas
20 x 21 inches

Odd/Even, 1990
sign paint on canvas
15.5 x 29 inches

The Forest for the Trees, 1990
wall painting
installation view, Center for Contemporary Art, Chicago, 1990

Untitled Grid (*Blue Queue; No Melon, No Lemon; Daredevil; Blue W;
Gray Yellow; Volkswagons Rust; Emblems; A Redder A; Anti-Titian;
Gray V; Felt Tip Pen; Look For (Spanish); Greyer G; Middle of Film
Noir; Green Genre Painting; Violetter*), 1990
sign paint and gouache on paper
sixteen sheets, each 20 x 30 inches; overall 84 x 124 inches

[bl]ueue	nomelon	daredevil	doubleu
grayello	rstuvw	mblmblm	a redder a
antititian	grayv	feltipen	buscar
greyerg	(lmno)	genre	violetter

Same, 1991
sign paint on canvas
7.5 x 23 inches

Stunts, 1991
sign paint on canvas
7.5 x 20 inches

Sisyphus, 1991
videotape, 7 min., 30 sec.

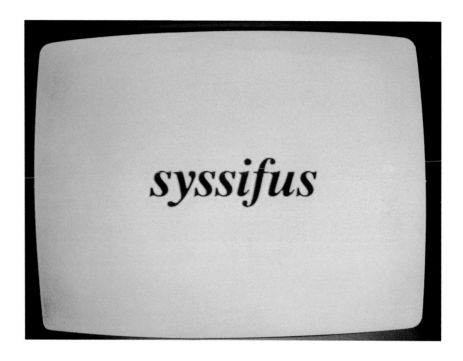

Corpus (*Cut Out; Four or Five; Missing in Action; Full Moon; Zone;*
Turn; Dr. Freud; Crescent Moon; Click; Mr. Dream Reader; Bloodclot;
Also Known as Kay; Sleeveless), 1992
sign paint on canvas
installation view, Laura Carpenter Gallery, Santa Fe, 1992

Deaf, 1993
sign paint on canvas
8 x 15.5 inches

Double Whammy, 1993
sign paint on canvas
10 x 50 inches

Still Life, 1993
sign paint on canvas
17.625 x 23.125 inches

FRUIT DISH

Tide, 1994
sign paint on canvas
25 x 33.5 inches

sirf girls
serf gerls
surf gurls

Star-Crossed, 1995
pencil on paper
12.5 x 13.5 inches

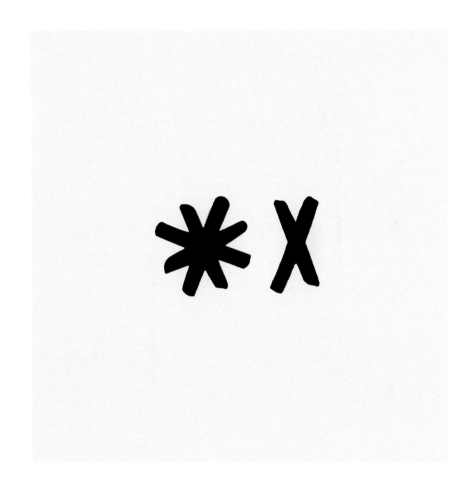

Back of the Boat, 1996
pencil on paper
12.25 x 20.25 inches

Leak, 1995
pencil on paper
15.25 x 22.75 inches

R(aft)

ROO F
FLOOR

Sheep in Wolf's Clothing, 1994
pencil on paper
14.625 x 21.125 inches

Dog Wood Bark, 1994
pencil on paper
15.5 x 16.5 inches

VIRGINia
WOOLf

dog
wood
BARK

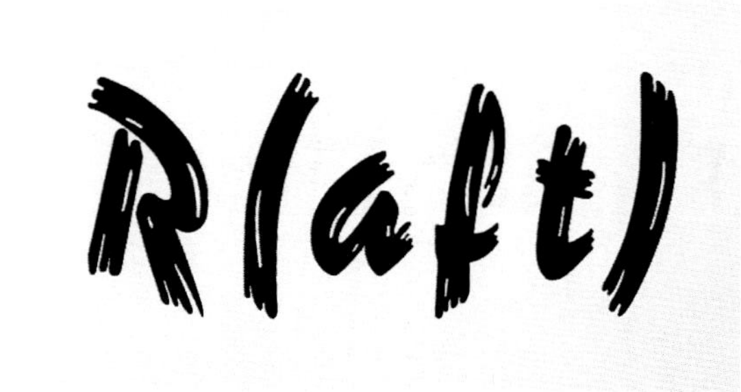

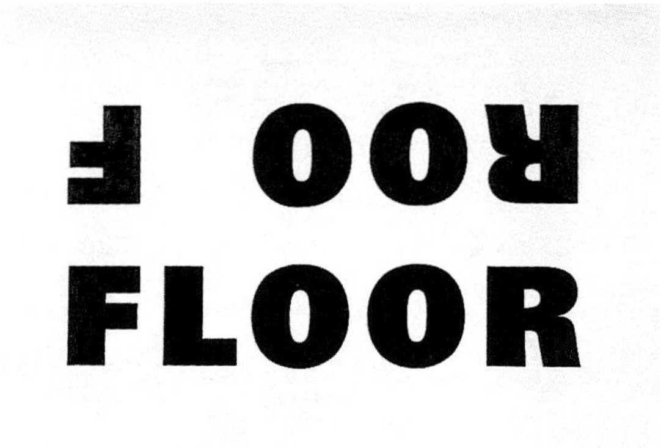

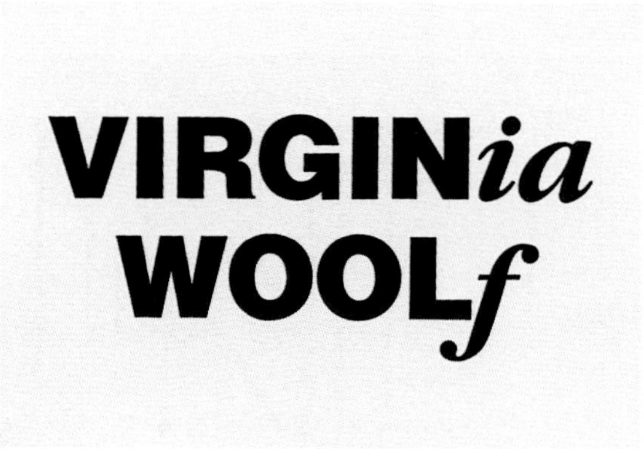

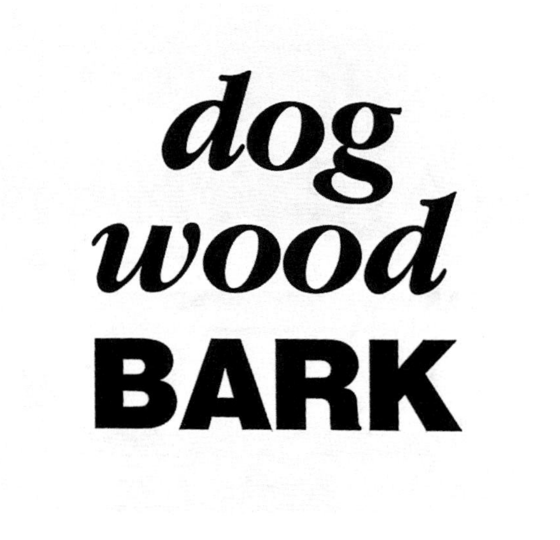

Bleed, 1996
marker on paper
12 x 27.25 inches

She-Man, 1996
wall painting
installation view, home of Ruth and Steve Durchslag

Surplus, 1996
sign paint on museum board
14.75 x 11.75 inches

Crotchety, 1997
sign paint on canvas
14 x 12 inches

Works in bold are exhibited at Otis.
Works in plain text are exhibited at MOCA.

Height precedes width precedes depth.

Carry On, Carrion
1972
Mixed media on paper
18 x 12 inches
Collection of the artist

Directions for a Man-Lady
1972
Mixed media on paper
18 x 12 inches
Collection of the artist

from Emily Post's Etiquette
1972
Colored pencil on paper
18 x 12 inches
Collection of the artist

Katherine Was Katherized and Katharsized
1972
Mixed media on paper
12 x 20 inches
Collection of the artist

The Virtue of Spaces
1972
Colored pencil on paper
18 x 12 inches
Collection of the artist

A Song and Dance
1978
Photographs, pen, and ink on paper
60 x 18 inches
Collection of the artist

Changing Seats
1978
Black-and-white photograph
60.5 x 45 inches
Collection of the artist

Gateway Park, Gary, Indiana II
1980
Photograph, ink, and china marker on paper
Two panels, each 20 x 24 inches
Collection of the artist

Hyde Park, Chicago, Illinois II
1980
Photograph, ink, and china marker on paper
Two panels, each 20 x 24 inches
Collection of the artist

Stairwalking: Directions/Patterns
1980
Ink and colored pencil on paper
44.25 x 58 inches
Collection of the artist

Stairwalking: Directions/Rhythms
1980
India ink, red ink, colored pencil, and black-and-white photograph on paper
23 x 14.5 inches
Collection of the artist

Stairwalking: Three Staircases
1980
Gelatin silver print
20 x 24 inches
Collection of the artist

Stairwalking: Up and Down
1981
India ink, colored pencil, and black-and-white photograph on paper
23 x 14.5 inches
Collection of the artist

No Noose Is Good Noose
1983
Painted plexiglas and masonite panels
168 x 62 x 26 inches
Collection of the artist

Border Peece
1984
Sign paint on museum board
14 x 21 x 6.5 inches
Private collection, Gary, Indiana

Alabama
1984
Sign paint on museum board
Two panels, each 17 x 11 inches
Collection of the artist

Eyesore
1984
Sign paint on museum board
17 x 11 inches
Collection of the artist

Honk if You're Foul
1984
Sign paint on museum board
17 x 11 inches
Collection of the artist

Leroy Was Here
1984
Sign paint on museum board
17 x 11 inches
Collection of the artist

Read Lips
1984
Sign paint on museum board
Three panels, each 17 x 11 inches
Helga Maria Klosterfelde, Hamburg

Sinking Feeling
1984
Sign paint on museum board
Two panels, each 17 x 11 inches
Collection of the artist

Skin Niks
1984
Sign paint on museum board
17 x 11 inches
Collection of the artist

Take a Bough
1984
Sign paint on museum board
17 x 11 inches
Collection of the artist

Glamour
1985
Sign paint on museum board
17 x 11 inches
Private collection. Courtesy Feature, Inc.,
New York

Blub, Blub, Blub
1985
Sign paint on museum board
Three panels, each 17 x 11 inches
Collection of the artist

Bam, Boo
1985
Sign paint on museum board and frame
Five panels, overall 18 x 60 inches
Collection of the artist

Big Talk
1985
Wall painting
132 x 210 inches
Collection of the artist

Various Strata
1986/96
Wall painting
101 x 99 inches
Collection of the artist

Classic Pairs II
1986
Sign paint on photocopy
23 x 24 inches
Collection of the artist

The Mexican Revolution
1986
Sign paint on photocopy
24 x 37.5 inches
Collection of the artist

Loin/Proche
1986
Sign paint on canvas
Two panels, each 11 x 14 inches
Laura Carpenter, Santa Fe, New Mexico

Jarred
1986
Sign paint on canvas
14 x 11 x 1.5 inches
Collection of the artist

No, Noah, Ah, Noah
1987
Sign paint on canvas
Two panels, each 14 x 11 x 2.25 inches
Collection of Rosenthal & Rosenthal,
New York

Edgar Degas
1987
Sign paint on canvas
Two panels, each 10 x 10 x 2.75 inches
Bodi Collection

Mr. Ed, Missed
1987
Sign paint on canvas
10 x 20 x 2.75 inches
Collection of the artist

Georgy, Porgy, Bess
1987
Sign paint on enamel
16 x 21 x 2.75 inches
Collection of the artist

Go on, Goon
1987
Sign paint on canvas
Four panels, each 10 x 10 x 2 inches
Collection of the artist

John Wilkes Booth
1987
Sign paint on canvas
20 x 20 inches
Collection Bill Arning

Six
1988
Sign paint on canvas and frame
14.25 x 17.5 inches
Private collection

*The "Ed" Paintings (Surprise; Technical
Difficulties; Sp-spit it Out; Blanks [two panels];
Ex-ed)*
1988
Sign paint on canvas
Six panels, each 32 x 20 inches
Collection of the artist

Tree-Lined Street
1989
Sign paint on canvas
16 x 10 inches
Anstiss and Ronald Krueck

White Elephant
1989
Sign paint on canvas
15 x 15 inches
Collection of Fredericka Hunter

Oh, Eau
1989/92
Silkscreened wall text, edition 5
Two panels, each 43 x 45.75 inches
Courtesy of the artist and Mark Patsfall
Graphics, Cincinnati

Little Statuette
1990
Sign paint on canvas
20 x 21 inches
Collection of Alvin D. Hall, New York

Odd/Even
1990
Sign paint on canvas
15.5 x 29 inches
Collection of the artist

You Lie Through Your Teeth
1990
Sign paint on canvas
7.75 x 19 inches
Private collection, London

The Forest for the Trees
1990
Wall painting
23.625 x 288 inches
Collection of the artist

*Untitled Grid (Blue Queue; No Melon, No
Lemon; Daredevil; Blue W; Gray Yellow;
Volkswagons Rust; Emblems; A Redder A;
Anti-Titian; Gray V; Felt Tip Pen; Look For
(Spanish); Greyer G; Middle of Film Noir;
Green Genre Painting; Violetter)*
1990
Sign paint and gouache on paper
Sixteen sheets, each 20 x 30 inches;
overall 84 x 124 inches
Collection of the artist

AIDS
1990/98
Offset on paper
Dimensions variable
Courtesy of the artist
Remade from bus poster on the occasion of
the MOCA/Otis exhibition by APLA, Los
Angeles

Out Of Order
1991
Sign paint on canvas
7.5 x 20.125 inches
Annette and Melvyn Klein

Same
1991
Sign paint on canvas
7.5 x 23 inches
Galerie Friedrich, Bern

Stunts
1991
Sign paint on canvas
7.5 x 20 inches
Collection of Chula Reynolds

Tidbit
1991
Sign paint on canvas
7.5 x 18 inches
Courtesy of the artist and Galerie Friedrich,
Bern

Partners
1991
Sign paint on canvas
Two panels, each 16 x 10 inches
The Progressive Corporation, Cleveland, Ohio

Sisyphus
1991
Videotape
7 min., 30 sec.
Collection of the artist

Corpus
1992
Corpus is an installation of the following
thirteen works:

Also Known as Kay
1992
Sign paint on canvas
7.5 x 21 inches
Collection of the artist

Bloodclot
1992
Sign paint on canvas
7.5 x 29 inches
From the Collection of Ginny
Williams

Click
1992
Sign paint on canvas
7.5 x 18 inches
From the Collection of Ginny
Williams

Crescent Moon
1992
Sign paint on canvas
7.5 x 21 inches
Private collection, New Mexico

Cut Out
1992
Sign paint on canvas
7.5 x 14 inches
Dr. James and Dorothy Stadler

Dr. Freud
1992
Sign paint on canvas
7.75 x 20.5 inches
Refco Group, LTD., New York

Four or Five
1992
Sign paint on canvas
7.5 x 20 inches
Mr. and Mrs. Robert J. Dodds III,
Santa Fe, New Mexico

Full Moon
1992
Sign paint on canvas
7.5 x 24 inches
Private collection, New Mexico

Missing in Action
1992
Sign paint on canvas
7.5 x 24 inches
Collection of the artist

Mr. Dream Reader
1992
Sign paint on canvas
7.75 x 35.5 inches
Refco Group, LTD., New York

Sleeveless
1992
Sign paint on canvas
7.75 x 40.5 inches
Private collection, New Mexico

Turn
1992
Sign paint on canvas
7.5 x 17 inches
Collection of the artist

Zone
1992
Sign paint on canvas
7.5 x 19 inches
Private collection, New Mexico

Deaf
1993
Sign paint on canvas
8 x 15.5 inches
Collection of A.G. Rosen, Wayne, New Jersey

Double Whammy
1993
Sign paint on canvas
10 x 50 inches
Collection of Eileen and Peter Norton,
Santa Monica

Little Sheep
1993
Sign paint on canvas
11 x 14 inches
Rosina Lee Yue

Still Life
1993
Sign paint on canvas
17.625 x 23.125 inches
Private collection, Philadelphia

Trickknees
1993
Sign paint on canvas
22.75 x 22.5 inches
Dr. Heinz Peter Hager, Bolzano, Italy

Phantom Limb
1993/96
Wall painting
180 x 261 inches
Collection of the artist

9/10
1993/94
Wall painting
180 x 129 inches
Collection of the artist

Aunt Bea
1994
Sign paint on canvas
25 x 30 inches
Margo and Bob Marbut

Dog Wood Bark
1994
Pencil on paper
15.5 x 16.5 inches
Anthony and Linda Grant, New York

Elvis, Elvis
1994
Sign paint on canvas
8 x 10 inches
Collection of Eileen and Peter Norton,
Santa Monica

Sheep in Wolf's Clothing
1994
Pencil on paper
14.625 x 21.125 inches
Collection Yvon Lambert, Montfauet,
France

Tide
1994
Sign paint on canvas
25 x 33.5 inches
Courtesy of the artist and Wooster
Gardens, New York

Leak
1995
Pencil on paper
15.25 x 22.75 inches
Collection Re Rebaudengo Sandretto, Turin

Star-Crossed
1995
Pencil on paper
12.5 x 13.5 inches
Courtesy Micah Lexier, Toronto

Back of the Boat
1996
Pencil on paper
12.25 x 20.25 inches
Courtesy of the artist and Wooster
Gardens, New York

Bleed
1996
Marker on paper
12 x 27.25 inches
Courtesy of the artist and Wooster
Gardens, New York

She-Man
1996
Wall painting
84 x 97 inches
From the Collection of Ruth and Steve
Durchslag

Surplus
1996
Sign paint on museum board
14.75 x 11.75 inches
Courtesy of the artist and Art:Concept,
Paris

Crotchety
1997
Sign paint on canvas
14 x 12 inches
Courtesy of the artist and Wooster
Gardens, New York

HI
1997/98
Wall painting
220 x 960 inches
Collection of the artist. Remade from billboard
on the occasion of the MOCA/Otis exhibition,
north wall, The Geffen Contemporary at
MOCA, Los Angeles

Kay Rosen

Born in Corpus Christi, Texas
Lives and works in Gary, Indiana

Education

B.A., Newcomb College of Tulane University, New Orleans, Louisiana
M.A., Northwestern University, Evanston, Illinois

Honors

National Endowment for the Arts, Visual Arts Grant, 1995
Awards in the Visual Arts 10, Fellowship, 1990
National Endowment for the Arts, Visual Arts Grant, 1989
National Endowment for the Arts, Visual Arts Grant, 1987

Selected Exhibition History

Individual Exhibitions and Projects

1998   "Kay Rosen: *lifeli[k]e*," The Museum of Contemporary Art, Los Angeles, and Otis Gallery,
            Otis College of Art and Design, Los Angeles (catalogue)
        "Kay Rosen: Girl Talk," Ten In One Gallery, Chicago
        "ABC (At Beaver College)," Beaver College Art Gallery, Glenside, Pennsylvania, in collaboration
            with Billboard Project, Center Gallery, Bucknell University, Lewisburg, Pennsylvania

1997   Galerie Michael Cosar, Düsseldorf
        "Kay Rosen: Short Stories/Tall Tales," MIT List Visual Arts Center, Cambridge, Massachusetts
            (catalogue)
        Wooster Gardens, New York

1996   Unlimited, Athens, Greece
        Art:Concept, Nice
        "Short Stories," Helga Maria Klosterfelde, Hamburg

1995   Galerie Friedrich, Bern
        Paul Morris Gallery, New York

1994   "Kay Rosen: Back Home in Indiana," Indianapolis Museum of Art, Indianapolis (catalogue)
        Richard Telles Fine Art, Los Angeles
        "Kay Rosen: Home on the Range," Museum of Contemporary Art, Chicago (catalogue)
        Galleria Massimo De Carlo, Milan

1993   Victoria Miro Gallery, London
       Feature, New York
       Jose Freire Fine Art, New York (two-person)

1992   Rhona Hoffman Gallery, Chicago
       Laura Carpenter Gallery, Santa Fe
       Feature, New York
       Cleveland Center for Contemporary Art, Cleveland

1991   Shoshana Wayne Gallery, Santa Monica
       "Manum de tabula," Shedhalle, Zurich (catalogue)
       Insam Gleicher Gallery, Chicago

1990   Feature, New York
       Victoria Miro Gallery, London (catalogue)
       Witte de With Center for Contemporary Art, Rotterdam

1989   Feature, New York

1988   Feature, New York
       Feature, Chicago

1987   Feature, Chicago

1986   "Kay Rosen: Lines on Lines," University Gallery of Fine Arts, Ohio State University, Columbus
       DePree Art Gallery, Hope College, Holland, Michigan

1984   Broadway Window, The New Museum of Contemporary Art, New York
       Feature, Chicago

1983   "Kay Rosen: Lines on Lines," Bertha Urdang Gallery, New York

1981   "Kay Rosen: Stairwalking: Notations/Diagrams," Bertha Urdang Gallery, New York

1980   "Kay Rosen: Photographic Performances," Franklin Furnace, New York

1979   "Kay Rosen: Photo-texts and Performances," Bertha Urdang Gallery, New York

Group Exhibitions

1998   "Points of Departure: Art on the Line," Main Line train station site-specific projects, Philadelphia
       "In the Beginning," Murray Guy, New York
       "The 3-D Project," Galerie Michael Cosar, Düsseldorf
       "Collective Visions," San Antonio Museum of Art, San Antonio
       "Pushing Boundaries: Lithographs from Nine American Fine Art Presses," Reed Gallery,
           University of Cincinnati, Cincinnati
       "A to Z: Language to be looked at and/or things to be read," The approach, London
       "Video Library," David Zwirner Gallery, New York
       "The End of the Line," Unlimited, Athens, Greece
       "Visions, 1998," Barry Whistler Gallery, Dallas
       "Edifying Sappho and Sophocles: A Ministry of Public Works Project," Sydney, Australia
       "Editions: General Idea, Christian Jankowski, Kay Rosen," Helga Maria Klosterfelde, Hamburg
       "Pierre Molinier, Kay Rosen, Kara Walker," Wooster Gardens, New York

1997   "Jingle Bells: A Project by 806," Galleria Massimo De Carlo, Milan
       "Druck & Graphik," Klosterfelde, Berlin
       "Critical Images: Conceptual Works from the 1960s to the Present," Leslie Tonkonow Gallery,
           New York
       "New Work," Feigen Gallery, Chicago
       "Frankensteinian," Caren Golden Fine Art, New York
       "From a Whisper to a Scream," Ten In One Gallery, Chicago

"Collections in Context: Recent Acquisitions," University Art Museum, University of California
    at Santa Barbara
"Point Mort," Art:Concept, Paris

1996   "Art in Chicago: 1945-1995," Museum of Contemporary Art, Chicago (catalogue)
"Preview," Galerie Michael Cosar, Düsseldorf
"Small Scale," Joseph Helman Gallery, New York
"Tangles," Otis Gallery, Otis College of Art and Design, Los Angeles
"Varietes," Le Capitou, Fréjus, France
"Thinking Print: Books to Billboards, 1980-95," The Museum of Modern Art, New York (catalogue)
"50x50x50x50," answering machines at various sites, London, organized by David Goldenberg
    and John Roberts
"Frankenstein (in Normal)," Illinois State University, Normal
"Mist," Hermetic Gallery, Milwaukee
"Second Sight: Modern Printmaking in Chicago," Block Gallery, Northwestern University,
    Evanston, Illinois (catalogue)
"Memento Mori," The Contemporary Arts Center, Cincinnati

1995   "Temporarily Possessed: The Semi-Permanent Collection," The New Museum of
    Contemporary Art, New York (catalogue)
"Word for Word," Beaver College Art Gallery, Glenside, Pennsylvania
"The Friendly Village," Milwaukee Institute of Art and Design, Milwaukee
"Art as Dramatic Comedy," Randolph Street Gallery, Chicago
"Tenth Anniversary Exhibition," Barry Whistler Gallery, Dallas
"Five Words or Less," Museum of Modern Art, Melbourne, Australia (catalogue)
"Murder," Bergamot Station, Los Angeles (catalogue)
"On Target," Horodner Romley Gallery, New York
"Altered States," Forum, St. Louis (catalogue)
"Pittura/Immedia: Malerei in den 90er Jahren," Neue Galerie am Landesmuseum Joanneum;
    and Künsterhaus Graz, Graz, Austria (catalogue)
"Representational Drawings," Feature, New York
"Zimmerdenkmaler," organized by Rafael von Uslar in various residential and commercial sites,
    Bochum, Germany (catalogue)

1994   "Small Paintings," Paul Morris Gallery, New York
"Scissors, Paper, Rock," Barry Whistler Gallery, Dallas
"Korrespondenzen/Correspondence," Berlinische Galerie, Martin Gropius-Bau, Berlin; and
    Chicago Cultural Center, Chicago (catalogue)
"Synesthesia: Sound and Vision in Contemporary Art," San Antonio Museum of Art, San Antonio
    (catalogue)
"The Use of Pleasure," Terrain, San Francisco (catalogue)

1993   "Beyond Loss: Art in the Era of AIDS," Washington Project for the Arts, Washington, D.C.
"Money," Nancy Drysdale Gallery, Washington, D.C.
"Surface Tension," Michael Klein Gallery, New York
"Post-Dialectical Index," Piazza Costanza, Trieste, Italy; La Tuatta Studio, Milan; and
    Horodner Romley Gallery, New York (catalogue)
"Words," Galerie Semmler at Galerie Jurgen Becker, Hamburg
"New Works," Feigen Gallery, Chicago
"Substitute Teachers," Sadie Bronfman Cultural Center, Montreal (catalogue)
"Legend in My Living Room," Rhona Hoffman Gallery, Chicago (catalogue)
"Is Poetry a Visual Art?," Turman Gallery, Indiana State University, Terre Haute (catalogue)

1992   "Small Talk," P.S. 1, New York; and Postmasters Gallery, New York
"Painting Culture," University of California at Irvine
"Artists' Books from the Permanent Collection," Museum of Contemporary Art, Chicago
"Why Paint?," The Renaissance Society at The University of Chicago, Chicago (catalogue)
"On Condition," Gallery 400, University of Illinois, Chicago
"Out of Bounds: The Word Becomes Art," Scottsdale Center for the Arts, Scottsdale, Arizona
Group exhibition, Jack Hanley Gallery, San Francisco
"Oh, Eau" Project, Rhona Hoffman Gallery, Chicago

Project with Michael Jenkins and Steven Evans, Andrea Rosen Gallery, New York
"Tattoo Collection," Air de Paris, Nice
"Multiples '92," Randolph Street Gallery, Chicago
"Twenty-fifth Anniversary Show," Bertha Urdang Gallery, New York
"Are You a Boy or Are You a Girl?," Real Art Ways, Hartford, Connecticut

1991   "At the End of the Day," Randy Alexander Gallery, New York
        "The Painted Word," Beth Urdang Fine Art, Boston
        "Candy Ass Carnival (When Good Things Happen to Loozers)," Stux Gallery, New York
        "Just What Is it that Makes Today's Homes So Different, So Appealing?" Hyde Collection,
            Great Falls, New York (catalogue)
        "Awards in the Visual Arts 10," Hirshhorn Museum and Sculpture Garden, Smithsonian Institution,
            Washington, D.C.; Albuquerque Museum; and Toledo Museum of Art, Toledo, Ohio (catalogue)
        "A New Low," Claudio Botello Gallery, Turin, Italy
        "Nine Is a Four-Letter Word (a letterpress project)," Key Gallery, Richmond, Virginia
        "Crude Thinking," MWMWM Gallery, Chicago
        "Lists," C.A.G.E., Cincinnati, Ohio
        "Something Pithier and More Psychological," Simon Watson Gallery, New York; and
            Meyers Bloom Gallery, Los Angeles
        "To Wit," Rosa Esman Gallery, New York
        "Directly on and off the Wall," Palm Beach Community College Museum of Art,
            Palm Beach, Florida
        "Women's Work," Victoria Miro Gallery, London
        "Five Artists," Marta Cevera Gallery, New York
        "News as Muse," School 33 Art Center, Baltimore
        "Artists in Words and #s," Wright State University Museum of Contemporary Art, Dayton, Ohio
            (catalogue)

1990   "In the Beginning . . .," Cleveland Center for Contemporary Art, Cleveland, Ohio
        "The Thing Itself," Feature, New York
        "Figure: See Feign," Center for Contemporary Art, Chicago
        "Work on Paper, An Invitational Exhibition," Paula Allen Gallery, New York
        "Word as Image: American Art 1960-1990," Milwaukee Art Museum; Oklahoma City Art Museum;
            and Contemporary Arts Museum, Houston (catalogue)
        "Art Against AIDS—On the Road," public project in five cities, organized by AMFAR
        "Five Installation Artists," Dart Gallery, Chicago
        "Broken Lines," Victoria Miro Gallery, London
        "Your Message Here" (billboard), Randolph Street Gallery, Chicago
        "The Clinic," Simon Watson Gallery, New York
        "Looking for Trouble," XS Gallery, Carson City, Nevada

1989   "AIDS: A Time Line 1979-1990" (a project by Group Material), University Art Museum,
            University of California at Berkeley; Wadsworth Atheneum, Hartford, Connecticut; and 1991
            Whitney Biennial, New York
        "Dorothy," Center for Contemporary Art, Chicago
        "Romancing the Stone," Feature, New York
        "Problems with Reading Rereading," Rhona Hoffman Gallery, Chicago
        "The Center Show," The Lesbian and Gay Community Services Center, New York (catalogue)

1988   "From Right to Left," Churchman Fehsenfeld Gallery, Indianapolis
        "Contention," New Langton Arts, San Francisco
        "Brave and Cruel," Randolph Street Gallery, Chicago
        "Information as Ornament," Feature, Chicago (catalogue)
        "Drawings," Robbin Lockett Gallery, Chicago
        "Plato's Cave," Greathouse Gallery, New York
        "Cartoon Like," Moming Dance and Arts Center, Chicago
        "Text Does Not Explain . . . ," Stux Gallery, Boston
        "The Language of Form, The Form of Language," Rosa Esman Gallery, New York
        "Romantic Distance," Jeffrey Neal Gallery, New York

1987   "Signs of Intelligent Life," Greathouse Gallery, New York

"New Chicago," Tangeman Fine Arts Gallery, University of Cincinnati
Group exhibition, Jan Baum Gallery, Los Angeles
"Wet Paint," Robbin Lockett Gallery, Chicago
Group exhibition, American Fine Arts, New York
"(Dark Laughter)," Randolph Street Gallery, Chicago
"The Non-spiritual in Art: Abstract Painting 1985-???," Feature, Chicago (catalogue)
"Nature," Feature, Chicago

1986 "Invitational Show of Women Artists," Feature Gallery, Chicago
"Cryptic Languages," Washington Project for the Arts, Washington, D.C.
"Non-spiritual America," CEPA Gallery, Buffalo, New York (catalogue)
"Promises, Promises," Feature, Chicago; and C.A.G.E., Cincinnati

1985 "National Artists Book Exhibit," Fifth Conference of Artists Organizations, Houston
"Critical Messages: The Use of Public Media for Political Art by Women," Artemesia Gallery,
    Chicago
"Messages from the Interior," N.A.M.E. Gallery, Chicago

1984 "Indiana Influence," Fort Wayne Museum of Art, Fort Wayne, Indiana (catalogue)

1983 "Window Shopping: An Art Exhibition in the Windows of 440 N. Wells St., 416-418 N. State St.,
    and 5 W. Hubbard St.," Chicago, organized by Kay Rosen and Margo Rush

1982 "Artists' Tribute to Bertha Urdang," Israel Museum, Jerusalem (catalogue)
"Tracking, Tracing, Marking, Pacing," Pratt Manhattan Gallery, New York; Sherman Gallery,
    Ohio State University; Anderson Gallery, University of Richmond, Virginia; and
    Washington Project for the Arts, Washington, D.C. (catalogue)

1981 "Bookworks: New Approaches to Artists' Books," Franklin Furnace, New York
"Ikons/Logos: Word as Image," Alternative Museum, New York

1980 "New Dimensions: Time," Museum of Contemporary Art, Chicago

1979 "Midway Between Comedy and Art," Midway Studios, University of Chicago

1978 "Daley's Tomb," N.A.M.E. Gallery, Chicago
"Paper Dolls," Moming Dance Center, Chicago

1977 "All Over the Place," Moming Dance Center, Chicago

Published Projects

Chicago Review 44, no. 2 (1998): front and back covers.

SURPLUS. A screensaver project by Camel Work In Progress, a Camel Cultural Initiative, 1998.

Myles, Eileen, *School of Fish.* Santa Rosa, Calif.: Black Sparrow Press, 1997, cover.

"Ripple Effects: Painting and Language," *New Observations*, no. 113 (Winter 1996): 18-19.

Permanent Food, no. 2, 1996, n.p.

Kahn, Robin, ed. *Time Capsule: A Concise Encyclopedia by Women Artists, Performers and Writers.*
    New York: Creative Time in cooperation with SOS Int'l, 1995, 415.

Art Muscle 10 (October/November 1995): cover.

Blocnotes (Paris), no. 8 (Winter 1995): 10-11.

Goethe Institute Chicago Newsletter, February-August 1995, cover.

Cottingham, Laura. *How many "bad" feminists does it take to change a lightbulb?.* New York: Sixty
    Percent Solution, 1994, 24.

White Walls (Chicago), nos. 33 & 34 (1994): n.p.

du (Zurich), no. 11 (November 1993): 15, 27, 34, 44, 50, 60, 68, 75, 78.

Kahn, Robin, ed. *Promotional Copy.* New York: M. Somerby, 1993.

L'endoit ideal: Un livre. Nice, France: L'Ile du roi, Centre d'art et jardin, Val de Reuil, 1993, 150-151.

The Progressive Corporation Annual Report 1991. Mayfield Heights, Ohio: The Progressive Corporation,
    1991, 7 unpaginated leaves inserted throughout.

Spunky International. New York: Billy Miller, 1992, back cover.

White Walls (Chicago), no. 30 (Summer 1992): n.p.

Bomb, no. 36 (Summer 1991): 97.

Dear World. San Francisco: Nayland Blake and Camille Roy, 1991, 72.

du (Zurich), no. 6 (June 1991): 58-61.

"AIDS: A Time Line (Group Material Project)," *Art in America* 78 (December 1990): 162-163.

Little Critic Pamphlet Three: Kay Rosen, paintings 1990. London: Victoria Miro Gallery, 1990.

Art Journal 49 (Summer 1990): 104-105.

White Walls (Chicago), no. 21 (Winter 1989): 29-31.

P-Form (Chicago), no. 12 (February-March 1989): cover, 6, 18.

File Magazine, no. 29 (1989): n.p.

Farm. Chicago: Feature and ICI, 1988, n.p.

Journal (Los Angeles Institute of Contemporary Art), no. 48 (Fall 1987): 8.

Farm. Chicago: Feature and ICI, 1987, back cover.

Reallife (New York), no. 15 (Winter 1995/86): 20-23.

White Walls (Chicago), no. 12 (Autumn 1985): 28-35.

Lines on Lines. Gary, Indiana: Self-published, 1982.

Format (Chicago) 2 (November 1979): 11.

Format (Chicago) 1 (December 1978): 1, 7.

Books, Exhibition Catalogues, and Periodicals

Adcock, Craig. "After Duchamp," *Tema Celeste*, no. 36 (Summer 1992): 50-53.

Artner, Alan. "Kay Rosen, Rhona Hoffman Gallery," *Chicago Tribune*, 6 November 1992, sec. 7, 38.

_____. "Is Painting Dead?," *Chicago Tribune*, 12 April 1992, 16.

_____. "Rosen's Smart Congenial Works Have a Way with Words," *Chicago Tribune*, 1 March 1991, sec. 7, 38.

_____. Review. *Chicago Tribune*, 17 March 1988, sec. 5, 14.

_____. Review. *Chicago Tribune*, 12 March 1987, sec. 5, 9F.

Bacigalupi, Don. *Synesthesia: Sound and Vision in Contemporary Art*. San Antonio: San Antonio Museum of Art, 1994.

Barnett, Rick, and Barbara Sahlman. *The Center Show*. New York: The Lesbian and Gay Community Services Center, 1989.

Bowman, Russell. *Word as Image: American Art 1960-1990*. Milwaukee: Milwaukee Art Museum, 1990.

Bright, Deborah. "New Dimensions: Time, Museum of Contemporary Art," *New Art Examiner* 7 (April 1980): 23.

Browning, Robert H. *Icons/Logos: Word as Image*. New York: Alternative Museum, 1981.

Brunetti, John. "Kay Rosen, Insam Gleicher Gallery," *New Art Examiner* 18 (May 1991): 44.

Byrum, John. "Kay Rosen, Cleveland Center for Contemporary Art," *New Art Examiner* 20 (November 1992): 33-34.

Calhoun, Sharon L. "Kay Rosen—Back Home in Indiana/Indianapolis Museum of Art." *Dialogue* 17 (November-December 1994): 25.

Cameron, Dan. *Just What Is it that Makes Today's Homes So Different, So Appealing?*. Great Falls, New York: Hyde Collection, 1991.

Chambers, Karen S. "Arts & Letters," *Upper and lower case* 23 (Summer 1996): 20-25.

Cotter, Holland. "Kay Rosen," *New York Times*, 21 April 1995, C19.

_____. "Kay Rosen, Bertha Urdang Gallery," *New York Arts Journal* (February 1979).

Collins, Tricia, and Richard Milazzo. *A New Low*. Turin: Claudio Botelo Gallery, 1991.

_____. *Non-spiritual America*. Buffalo, New York: CEPA Gallery, 1986.

Day, Holliday T. *Kay Rosen: Back Home in Indiana*. Indianapolis: Indianapolis Museum of Art, 1994.

Donohoe, Victoria. "Kay Rosen: Beaver College," *Philadelphia Inquirer*, 1 March 1998, MC2.

English, Christopher. "De-merchandising Art: Shopping for an Alternative," *New Art Examiner* 10 (Summer 1983): 13.

Farley, Belinda L. "Sign Language Gets Positive Greeting: Bucknell University Puts Indiana Artist's Work to Road Test," *The Daily Item* (Susquehanna Valley, Penn.), 24 January 1998, A1.

Frank, Peter. *Indiana Influence*. Fort Wayne: Fort Wayne Museum of Art, 1984.

F[rankel], D[avid]. "Kay Rosen: lifeli[k]e," *Artforum* 37 (September 1998): 41.

Frueh, Joanna. *Narrative Imagery: Tell Me a Story*. Chicago: ARC Gallery, 1979.

Gerber, Elizabeth. "Bern: Kay Rosen in der Galerie Erika • Otto Friedrich," *Kunst-Bulletin*, no. 7/8 (July-August 1995): 36.

Gillick, Liam. "Kay Rosen, Victoria Miro," *Artscribe*, no. 85 (January-February 1991): 76.

Goldfarb, Brian, John Hatfield, Laura Trippi, and Mimi Young. *Temporarily Possessed: The Semi-Permanent Collection*. New York: The New Museum of Contemporary Art, 1995.

Goley, Mary Anne. *Money: Medium and Message*. Washington, D.C.: Nancy Drysdale Gallery, 1993.

Gregos, Katerina. "Kay Rosen: Unlimited, Athens, Greece," *Zing Magazine* 2 (Winter 1998): 157.

_____. "Kay Rosen, Unlimited Gallery," *Art Net* (Athens), no. 4 (Summer 1997): 72.

Grout, Catherine. "Manum de Tabula: Zurich, Shedhalle," *Arte Factum*, no. 42 (February-March 1992): 48.

Hixson, Kathryn. "Kay Rosen, Rhona Hoffman Gallery," *Flash Art*, no. 168 (January-February 1993): 94.

_____. "Chicago in Review" (Kay Rosen, Insam Gleicher Gallery), *Arts Magazine* 65 (May 1991): 106.

_____. "AVA 10: 1991." In *Awards in the Visual Arts 10*. Washington, D.C.: Hirshhorn Museum and Sculpture Garden, Smithsonian Institution, 1991.

_____. "Chicago in Review" (Dorothy, Center for Contemporary Art), *Arts Magazine* 64 (November 1989): 109-110.

Hoffberg, Judith A. "Lines on Lines by Kay Rosen," *Umbrella* 6 (March 1983): 50.

Horodner, Stuart. "Spellcheck," *Surface*, no. 10 (1997): 24.

_____. *Substitute Teachers*. Montreal: Sadie Bronfman Cultural Center, 1993.

Hudson, Richard Bretell, and Kevin Maginnis. *The Non-spiritual in Art: Abstract Painting 1985-???*. Chicago: Feature, 1987.

Janneke, Wesseling. "Review, Witte de With," *NRC Handelsblad CS*, 31 October 1990, 5.

Jocks, H.N. "Kay Rosen: Summoning Lust for Lettering," *Westdeutsch Zeitung*, 18 October 1997.

Johnson, Ken. "The Painted Word," *Vogue* (August 1991): 142-148.

Kandel, Susan. "Wonderful Tinkering by Rosen," *Los Angeles Times*, 28 October 1994, F23.

_____. "Kay Rosen, Shoshana Wayne Gallery," *Los Angeles Times*, 13 December 1991, F24.

Kirshner, Judith Russi. "read read rosens," *Artforum* 29 (December 1990): cover, 91-95.

_____, and Gregory Knight. *Korrespondenzen/Correspondences*. Berlin: Berlinische Galerie, Martin Gropius Bau; and Chicago: Chicago Cultural Center, 1994.

Lieberman, Rhonda. "Recent Painting by Jewish Woman in Indiana," *Art·Text*, no. 46 (September 1993): 54-59.

_____. "Kay Rosen, Feature," *Artforum* 30 (April 1992): 95.

Lux, Harm. *Manum de tabula*. Zurich: Shedhalle, 1991.

Macchi, Catherine. "Kay Rosen, Art Concept," *Blocnotes*, no. 14 (January-February 1997): 127.

Mahoney, Robert. "New York in Review (Kay Rosen, Feature)," *Arts Magazine* 65 (January 1991): 102-105.

Martin, Abbe. "Artists Honor Daley: A Monumental Undertaking," *The Reader* (Chicago), 10 March 1978, 7.

McCracken, David. "'Information as Ornament' tests the limits," *Chicago Tribune*, 22 July 1988, sec. 7, 59.

McDaniel, Craig. *Is Poetry a Visual Art?*. Terre Haute, Indiana: Turman Art Gallery, Indiana State University, 1993.

Morgan, Robert. *Post-Dialectical Index*. Trieste: Piazza Costanza; and Milan: La Tuatta Studio, 1993.

Morgan, Stuart. "Kay Rosen, Victoria Miro Gallery," *Time Out* (London), 3-10 October 1990, 57.

Myers, Terry R. "Kay Rosen: A Picture of a Word Is Worth More Than a Thousand Words." In Judith Kirshner and Gregory Knight, *Korrespondenzen/ Correspondences*. Berlin: Berlinische Galerie, Martin Gropius Bau; and Chicago: Chicago Cultural Center, 1994, 106, 108.

_____. "Painting Camp: The Subculture of Painting, The Mainstream of Decoration," *Flash Art*, no. 179 (November-December 1994): 73-76.

_____. "Kay Rosen," *Blocnotes*, no. 5 (Winter 1994): 68-69.

_____. "Kay Rosen," *Arts Magazine* 66 (April 1992): 75.

Myles, Eileen. "Prints of Words," *Print Collectors Newsletter* 24 (September-October 1993): 132-135.

Nickas, Robert. *The Use of Pleasure*. San Francisco: Terrain, 1994.

_____, and Jeanne Greenberg. *Altered States*. St. Louis: Forum, 1995.

Nikkei Art (April 1992): 188-189.

Norris, Tim. "Kay Rosen, M.I.T. List Visual Arts Center," *New Art Examiner* 25 (September 1997): 61.

Pagel, David. *Why Paint?*. Chicago: The Renaissance Society at The University of Chicago, 1992.

Palmer, Laurie. "Problems with Reading/Rereading, Rhona Hoffman Gallery," *Artforum* 28 (September 1989): 151.

Porges, Tim. "Kay Rosen, Museum of Contemporary Art," *New Art Examiner* 22 (November 1994): 39.

Raynor, Vivian. "Kay Rosen/Kay Walkingstick, Bertha Urdang Gallery," *New York Times*, 19 June 1981, C20.

Reid, Graeme. "The Language of Art," *Arts Indiana* 17 (March 1995): 30.

Renton, Andrew. "Kay Rosen," *Blitz* (December 1990): 34.

Riddell, Jennifer. *Kay Rosen: Short Stories/Tall Tales*. Cambridge, Massachusetts: M.I.T. List Visual Arts Center, 1997.

Robbins, David, and Kevin Maginnis. *Information as Ornament*. Chicago: Feature, 1988.

Robinson, Walter. "State of the Art: Young, Gifted, and Affordable," *Metropolitan Home*, November 1987, 58-70.

Rosenberg, Barry. *Artists in Words and #s*. Dayton, Ohio: Wright State University Museum of Contemporary Art, 1991.

Rubinstein, Raphael. "Full Circle," *Art in America* 83 (May 1995): 108-109.

Ryan, Dinah. "Nine Is a Four-Letter Word, Key Gallery," *New Art Examiner* 19 (December 1991): 41.

Scanlan, Joseph. "Problems with Reading Rereading, Rhona Hoffman Gallery," *Artscribe*, no. 77 (September-October 1989): 84-85.

_____. "Kay Rosen, Feature," *Dialogue* 11 (July-August 1988): 33-34.

Schwartz, Ellen. *Tracking, Tracing, Marking, Pacing*. New York: Pratt Manhattan Gallery, 1982.

Seidel, Miriam. "Kay Rosen at Beaver College Art Gallery," *Art in America* 86 (October 1998): 141-143.

Shaneff, Angela. "Kay Rosen Draws on Words (interview)," *Indiana Arts Commission Quarterly* (Summer 1988): 4.

Sharpless, Greg. "Annual Reports with a Fine Arts Edge," *Step By Step Graphics*, Spring 1993, 82-91.

Smith, Roberta. "The Group Show as Crystal Ball," *New York Times*, 6 July 1990, C1, C23.

Sozanski, Edward J. "Kay Rosen: Showing that ABC Isn't So Simple After All," *Philadelphia Inquirer*, 6 March 1998, 36.

Spector, Buzz. "Kay Rosen, Feature," *Artforum* 26 (May 1988): 154.

Steimer, Flora. "Pionierstaak waargemaakt," *Algereen Dagblad* (Rotterdam), 31 October 1990.

Tamblyn, Christine. "All Over the Place," *New Art Examiner* 4 (June 1977): 9.

Thompson, Mark. "Kay Rosen, Ed Ruscha," *Art Monthly* (London), no. 141 (November 1990): 22-23.

Urdang, Bertha. *Artists Tribute to Bertha Urdang*. Jerusalem: Israel Museum, 1982.

Upton, Kim. "When a Building on State St. Talks, People Say: 'Huh?,'" *Chicago Sun Times*, 23 June 1983, 59.

Vacca, Linnea B. "Words, Words, Words," *Arts Indiana* 13 (May 1991): 24-27.

Van De Walle, Mark. "Kay Rosen, Laura Carpenter Gallery," *THE Magazine* (Santa Fe) (October 1992): 17.

Van der Craats, Christopher. *Five Words or Less.* Melbourne, Australia: Museum of Modern Art, 1995.

Von Ralf, Poerschke. "Vom Mangel der Sprache—Short Stories: Kay Rosen in der Galerie Klosterfelde,"
	Hamburger Rundschau, no. 39 (19 September 1996).

Von Uslar, Rafael. *Zimmerdenkmaler.* Essen, Germany: Klartext Verlag, 1995.

Warren, Lynne. *Art in Chicago: 1945-1995.* Chicago: Museum of Contemporary Art; and New York: Thames
	and Hudson, 1996, 136, 214, 279-280.

Wasserman, Nadine. *Kay Rosen: Home on the Range.* Chicago: Museum of Contemporary Art, 1994.

Weibel, Peter. *Pittura/Immedia: Malerei in dem 90er Jahren.* Klagenfurt, Austria: Verlag Ritter Klagenfurt,
	1995.

Wittig, Rob. "Kay Rosen, Feature," *Art in America* 77 (January 1989): 157.

Wye, Deborah. *Thinking Print: Books to Billboards, 1980-95.* New York: The Museum of Modern Art, 1996.

Yau, John. *Murder.* Santa Monica: Smart Art Press, 1995.

Yood, James. *Second Sight: Modern Printmaking in Chicago.* Evanston, Illinois: Block Gallery,
	Northwestern University, 1996.

AIDS, 1990
fifty bus tailgate posters, Chicago
project in five cities for Art Against AIDS on the Road,
sponsored by AMFAR